EASY MONEY

WILLIAM MARTIN

Names: Martin, William Thomas, 1955- author. Title: Easy money / by William Martin. Description: Upper Darby, PA : William Martin, [2023] Identifiers: ISBN: 979-8-218-24517-7 | LCCN: 2023914765 Subjects: LCSH: Finance, Personal. | Financial literacy. | Investments. | Portfolio management. | Interpersonal relations. | Communication. | Emotional maturity. | Critical thinking. | Vocational guidance. | Life skills--Handbooks, manuals, etc. | LCGFT: Self-help publications. Classification: LCC: HG179 | DDC: 332/.024--dc23

Library of Congress Control Number:2023914765

CONTENTS

INTRODUCTION

There are many things that we learn in school, but there are also many things that we don't. Some of these things are essential for our personal and professional growth, but they are often overlooked or ignored by the traditional education system. In this book, I will introduce you to some of the topics that they did not teach us in school, such as emotional intelligence, financial literacy, critical thinking, creativity, and more. I will also share with you some of the strategies and resources that you can use to learn these skills on your own and apply them to your life. By the end of this book, you will have a better understanding of yourself and the world around you. You will be able to achieve your goals and dreams with more confidence and ease. The book has essential skills and lessons to help you thrive at work, home and relationships.

It's not just a book, it is a road map to success. The book is filled with practical tips and strategies for achieving financial stability. You will learn how to tap into your creativity and use it to achieve your goals. It has Crucially important life skills that are not taught in schools, this is why so many people end of suffering for most of their lives. You will also discover secrets to a happy and successful life

HOW TO BECOME RICH ON A LOW SALARY

It is possible to become rich on a low salary, but it requires dedication, hard work, and a lot of planning. It is not an easy task, but it is possible. With the right strategies and a bit of luck, anyone can become wealthy on a low salary.

WHAT IS A LOW SALARY?

A low salary is defined as any salary that is below the median income for a given area. The median income is the amount of money that half of the population earns more than and half of the population earns less than. In the United States, the median income is around $60,000 per year. Therefore, any salary that is below this amount would be considered a low salary.

HOW TO BECOME RICH ON A LOW SALARY

Becoming rich on a low salary is possible, but it requires dedication and hard work. Here are some tips to help you get started:

1. **Live Below Your Means:** The first step to becoming rich on a low salary is to live below your means. This means that you should not spend more money than you make. This can be difficult, especially if you are used to

living a certain lifestyle, but it is essential if you want to become wealthy.

2. **Invest Wisely:** Investing is one of the best ways to become rich on a low salary. Investing your money wisely can help you grow your wealth over time. Investing in stocks, bonds, mutual funds, and other investments can help you build wealth over time.

3. **Save Money:** Saving money is another important step to becoming rich on a low salary. Saving money can help you build an emergency fund, which can be used in case of an unexpected expense. It can also help you save for retirement or other long-term goals.

4. **Start a Side Hustle:** Starting a side hustle can be a great way to make extra money on a low salary. A side hustle can be anything from freelancing to selling products online. It can help you make extra money to invest or save.

5. **Take Advantage of Tax Breaks:** Taking advantage of tax breaks can help you save money on your taxes. This can help you save money and invest more of your income.

BENEFITS OF BECOMING RICH ON A LOW SALARY

There are many benefits to becoming rich on a low salary. Here are some of the most common benefits:

1. Financial Security: Becoming rich on a low salary can provide you with financial security. This means that you will have enough money to cover your basic needs and have some extra money to save or invest.

2. **Freedom:** Becoming rich on a low salary can give you the freedom to do what you want with your money.

You can use your money to travel, buy a house, or start a business.

3. **Security:** Becoming rich on a low salary can provide you with security. This means that you will have enough money to cover your basic needs and have some extra money to save or invest.

CONCLUSION

Becoming rich on a low salary is possible, but it requires dedication and hard work. It is important to live below your means, invest wisely, save money, start a side hustle, and take advantage of tax breaks. These strategies can help you become wealthy on a low salary.

Q: How much money do I need to become rich on a low salary?

A: The amount of money you need to become rich on a low salary depends on your goals and lifestyle. Generally, it is recommended to save at least 10% of your income and invest the rest.

Q: What is the best way to invest my money?

A: The best way to invest your money depends on your goals and risk tolerance. Generally, it is recommended to diversify your investments and invest in a mix of stocks, bonds, mutual funds, and other investments.

Q: How can I save money on a low salary?

A: There are several ways to save money on a low salary. You can start by living below your means and cutting back on unnecessary expenses. You can also take advantage of tax breaks and look for ways to save money on everyday purchases.

Q: What is the best way to start a side hustle?

A: The best way to start a side hustle depends on your skills and interests. You can start by researching different side hustles and finding one that fits your skills and interests. You can also look for ways to monetize your hobbies or skills.

Q: What are the benefits of becoming rich on a low salary?

A: The benefits of becoming rich on a low salary include financial security, freedom, and security. Financial security means that you will have enough money to cover your basic needs and have some extra money to save or invest. Freedom means that you can do what you want with your money. Security means that you will have enough money to cover your basic needs and have some extra money to save or invest.

HOW TO MAKE $100 A DAY: A COMPREHENSIVE GUIDE

INTRODUCTION

Making money online is a great way to supplement your income or even replace it entirely. With the right strategies and dedication, you can make $100 a day or more. In this comprehensive guide, we'll show you how to make $100 a day with a variety of methods.

AFFILIATE MARKETING

Affiliate marketing is one of the most popular ways to make money online. It involves promoting products or services from other companies and earning a commission when someone makes a purchase. To get started, you'll need to find a reputable affiliate program and sign up. Once you're approved, you can start promoting the products or services and earning commissions.

FREELANCE WRITING

Freelance writing is another great way to make money online. You can write articles, blog posts, web content, and more for clients. To get started, you will need to create a portfolio of your work and start pitching it to potential clients. Once you land a few clients, you can start earning money for your writing.

SELLING DIGITAL PRODUCTS

If you have a skill or knowledge that you can share, you can create digital products such as 11, courses, or templates and sell them online. You can create the products yourself or outsource the work to someone else. Once you have the products ready, you can start selling them and earning money.

SELLING PHYSICAL PRODUCTS

If you'd rather sell physical products, you can do that too. You can create your own products or source them from a wholesaler. You can then list them on an online marketplace such as Amazon or eBay and start selling. You'll need to factor in the cost of shipping and handling when pricing your products.

DROPSHIPPING

Dropshipping is another great way to make money online. With dropshipping, you don't have to worry about stocking or shipping products. Instead, you partner with a dropshipping supplier who handles all of that for you. You just need to list the products on your website and take orders. When someone orders, the supplier ships the product directly to the customer.

ONLINE SURVEYS

Online surveys are a great way to make a few extra dollars in your spare time. There are a variety of survey sites that you can sign up for and start taking surveys. You won't make a lot of money, but it's a great way to make a few extra dollars.

INVESTING

Investing is another great way to make money. You can invest in stocks, bonds, mutual funds, and more. You'll need to do your research and understand the risks before investing. But if you're willing to take the risk, investing can be a great way to make money.

YOUTUBE

YouTube is a great platform for making money. You can create videos and upload them to YouTube. You can then monetize your videos with ads and start earning money. You can also create a YouTube channel and promote products or services to your viewers.

CONCLUSION

Making $100 a day is possible with the right strategies and dedication. There are a variety of methods you can use to make money online, from affiliate marketing to selling digital products. With the right approach, you can make $100 a day or more.

Q: How much money can I make with affiliate marketing?

A: The amount of money you can make with affiliate marketing depends on the products or services you're promoting and the amount of traffic you're able to generate. With the right strategies, you can make a significant amount of money.

Q: How do I get started with freelance writing?

A: To get started with freelance writing, you'll need to create a portfolio of your work and start pitching to potential clients. You can also look for freelance writing jobs on job boards or freelance marketplaces.

Q: What is dropshipping?

A: Dropshipping is a business model where you partner with a dropshipping supplier who handles all of the stocking and shipping of products for you. You just need to list the products on your website and take orders.

Q: How much money can I make with online surveys?

A: The amount of money you can make with online surveys depends on the number of surveys you take and the amount you're paid per survey. You won't make a lot of money, but it's a great way to make a few extra dollars.

Q: What is the best way to make money with YouTube?

A: The best way to make money with YouTube is to create videos and monetize them with ads. You can also create a

YouTube channel and promote products or services to your viewers.

DO THIS TO BECOME WEALTHY

INTRODUCTION

Wealth is something that many people strive for, but few ever achieve. It is a goal that requires dedication, hard work, and a willingness to take risks. But it is also something that can be achieved with the right strategies and tactics. In this article, we will discuss the steps you can take to become wealthy and achieve financial freedom.

WHAT IS WEALTH?

Wealth is the accumulation of assets that can be used to generate income or provide security. It is not just about having a lot of money, but also having the right investments and strategies in place to ensure that your wealth is protected and grows over time.

WHY DO YOU WANT TO BECOME WEALTHY?

The reasons for wanting to become wealthy vary from person to person. Some people want to be able to provide for their family, while others want to be able to travel and enjoy life without worrying about money. Whatever your reasons, it is important to have a clear goal in mind when you are setting out to become wealthy.

WHAT ARE THE STEPS TO BECOMING WEALTHY?

The steps to becoming wealthy are not complicated, but they do require dedication and hard work. Here are the steps you should take to become wealthy:

1. Set a Goal: The first step to becoming wealthy is to set a goal. This goal should be specific and measurable, and it should be something that you are passionate about.
2. Create a Plan: Once you have set a goal, you need to create a plan to achieve it. This plan should include a budget, an investment strategy, and a timeline for achieving your goal.
3. Invest Wisely: Investing is one of the most important steps to becoming wealthy. You should invest in assets that have the potential to generate income and appreciate in value over time.
4. Live Below Your Means: Living below your means is essential to becoming wealthy. This means spending less than you earn and saving the difference.
5. Take Risks: Taking risks is an important part of becoming wealthy. You should be willing to take calculated risks in order to achieve your goals.
6. Stay Focused: Staying focused on your goal is essential to becoming wealthy. You should stay focused on your goal and not be distracted by short-term gains.

WHAT ARE THE BENEFITS OF BECOMING WEALTHY?

The benefits of becoming wealthy are numerous. Wealth can provide financial security, freedom, and the ability to pursue your passions. It can also provide you with the opportunity to give back to your community and make a positive impact on the world.

CONCLUSION

Becoming wealthy is not an easy task, but it is achievable with dedication and hard work. By setting a goal, creating a plan, investing wisely, living below your means, taking risks, and staying focused, you can achieve financial freedom and become wealthy.

Q: How long does it take to become wealthy?

A: The amount of time it takes to become wealthy depends on your goals, your plan, and your dedication. It can take anywhere from a few months to several years to become wealthy.

Q: What is the best way to invest money?

A: The best way to invest money depends on your goals and risk tolerance. Generally, it is best to diversify your investments and invest in assets that have the potential to generate income and appreciate in value over time.

Q: How can I save money to become wealthy?

A: The best way to save money to become wealthy is to live below your means and save the difference. You should also create a budget and stick to it in order to ensure that you are saving as much as possible.

Q: What are the risks of becoming wealthy?

A: The risks of becoming wealthy include the potential for financial losses, the possibility of being taken advantage of, and the potential for increased stress. It is important to be aware of these risks and take steps to mitigate them.

Q: What is the best way to stay motivated when trying to become wealthy?

A: The best way to stay motivated when trying to become wealthy is to set realistic goals and to track your progress. You should also reward yourself for reaching milestones and celebrate your successes.

HOW TO MAKE MONEY IN THE STOCK MARKET

Making money in the stock market is a goal that many people have, but few understand how to achieve it. Investing in stocks can be a great way to build wealth over time, but it is important to understand the basics of stock investing before diving in. This article will provide an overview of the stock market, explain the different types of stocks, and provide tips on how to make money in the stock market.

WHAT IS THE STOCK MARKET?

The stock market is a collection of exchanges where stocks, bonds, and other securities are bought and sold. It is a global network of buyers and sellers, and it is the primary way that companies raise capital. When a company wants to raise money, it will issue shares of stock, which are then traded on the stock market.

TYPES OF STOCKS

There are two main types of stocks: common stocks and preferred stocks. Common stocks are the most common type of stock and represent ownership in a company. Preferred stocks are a type of stock that gives the holder certain rights, such as the right to receive dividends before common stockholders.

HOW TO INVEST IN STOCKS

Investing in stocks can be a great way to build wealth over time, but it is important to understand the basics of stock investing before diving in. The first step is to open a brokerage account, which is an account that allows you to buy and sell stocks. Once you have opened an account, you can start researching stocks and making trades.

STRATEGIES FOR MAKING MONEY IN THE STOCK MARKET

There are several strategies that can be used to make money in the stock market. One of the most popular strategies is to buy and hold stocks for the long term. This strategy involves buying stocks and holding them for a long period of time, such as several years. Another popular strategy is to buy and sell stocks quickly, which is known as day trading.

TIPS FOR INVESTING IN STOCKS

When investing in stocks, it is important to understand the risks involved. Investing in stocks can be a great way to build wealth over time, but it is important to understand the basics of stock investing before diving in. It is also important to diversify your investments, which means investing in different types of stocks and other investments. Finally, it is important to do your research and understand the company you are investing in.

CONCLUSION

Investing in the stock market can be a great way to build wealth over time, but it is important to understand the basics of stock investing before diving in. It is important to do your research and understand the company you are investing in, as well as diversify your investments and understand the risks involved. With the right strategies and tips, you can make money in the stock market.

Q: What is the stock market?

A: The stock market is a collection of exchanges where stocks, bonds, and other securities are bought and sold. It is a global network of buyers and sellers, and it is the primary way that companies raise capital.

Q: What are the different types of stocks?

A: There are two main types of stocks: common stocks and preferred stocks. Common stocks are the most common type of stock and represent ownership in a company. Preferred stocks are a type of stock that gives the holder certain rights, such as the right to receive dividends before common stockholders.

Q: How do I invest in stocks?

A: The first step is to open a brokerage account, which is an account that allows you to buy and sell stocks. Once you have opened an account, you can start researching stocks and making trades.

Q: What strategies can I use to make money in the stock market?

A: There are several strategies that can be used to make money in the stock market. One of the most popular strategies is to buy and hold stocks for the long term. This strategy involves buying stocks and holding them for a long period of time, such as several years. Another popular strategy is to buy and sell stocks quickly, which is known as day trading.

Q: What tips should I follow when investing in stocks?

A: When investing in stocks, it is important to understand the risks involved. It is also important to diversify your investments, which means investing in different types of stocks and other investments. Finally, it is important to do your research and understand.

HOW TO INVEST YOUR FIRST $1000

Investing your first $1000 can be a daunting task. With so many options available, it can be difficult to know where to start. Fortunately, there are some simple steps you can take to ensure that your money is invested wisely and that you get the most out of your investment. In this article, we will discuss the basics of investing, the different types of investments available, and how to get started.

THE BASICS OF INVESTING

Before you can begin investing, it is important to understand the basics of investing. Investing is the process of putting money into an asset with the expectation of making a return on your investment. Investing can be done in a variety of ways, including stocks, bonds, mutual funds, real estate, and more.

When investing, it is important to understand the risks associated with each type of investment. Investing in stocks, for example, carries more risk than investing in bonds. It is also important to understand the different types of investments and how they work.

TYPES OF INVESTMENTS

When it comes to investing your first $1000, there are a variety of options available. The most common types of investments include stocks, bonds, mutual funds, real estate, and more.

- Stocks: Stocks are shares of ownership in a company. When you buy a stock, you are buying a piece of the company. When the company does well, the stock price increases, and when the company does poorly, the stock price decreases.
- Bonds: Bonds are loans that are made to a company or government. When you buy a bond, you are lending money to the company or government. The company or government pays you interest on the loan, and when the bond matures, you get your money back.
- Mutual Funds: Mutual funds are a type of investment that pools money from many investors and invests it in a variety of stocks, bonds, and other investments. Mutual funds are managed by professional money managers who make decisions about which investments to buy and sell.
- Real Estate: Real estate is a type of investment that involves buying and selling property. Real estate can be a great way to make money, but it also carries a lot of risk.

HOW TO GET STARTED

Once you have a basic understanding of the different types of investments available, it is time to start investing your first $1000. The first step is to decide how you want to invest your money. Do you want to invest in stocks, bonds, mutual funds, or real estate?

Once you have decided on the type of investment you want to make, it is time to start researching. Researching the different types of investments and the companies or funds you are interested in is essential to making a wise investment decision.

Once you have done your research, it is time to start investing. You can open an account with a broker or an online investment platform and start investing your money.

CONCLUSION

Investing your first $1000 can be a daunting task. However, with the right research and understanding of the different types of investments available, you can make a wise decision and get the most out of your investment.

Q: What is the best way to invest my first $1000?

A: The best way to invest your first $1000 depends on your individual goals and risk tolerance. Generally speaking, stocks, bonds, mutual funds, and real estate are all good options for investing your first $1000.

Q: How do I start investing?

A: The first step to investing is to decide which type of investment you want to make. Once you have decided, you can open an account with a broker or an online investment platform and start investing your money.

Q: What is the risk associated with investing?

A: All investments carry some degree of risk. The amount of risk depends on the type of investment you make. Stocks, for example, carry more risk than bonds. It is important to understand the risks associated with each type of investment before you start investing.

Q: What is the difference between stocks and bonds?

A: Stocks are shares of ownership in a company. When you buy a stock, you are buying a piece of the company. Bonds are loans that are made to a company or government. When you buy a bond, you are lending money to the company or government.

THE ONLY 6 ETFS YOU'LL NEED TO BECOME A MILLIONAIRE

Exchange-traded funds (ETFs) are a great way to diversify your portfolio and get exposure to a wide range of asset classes. But with so many ETFs available, it can be difficult to know which ones to choose. In this article, we'll look at the six ETFs you'll need to become a millionaire.

WHAT ARE ETFS?

ETFs are investment funds that are traded on stock exchanges. They are similar to mutual funds in that they are composed of a basket of securities, such as stocks, bonds, and commodities. However, unlike mutual funds, ETFs are traded throughout the day on stock exchanges, just like stocks. This makes them more liquid and easier to buy and sell.

BENEFITS OF INVESTING IN ETFS

ETFs offer a number of benefits to investors. They are typically low-cost, diversified, and tax efficient. They also provide access to a wide range of asset classes, such as stocks, bonds, commodities, and currencies. Additionally, ETFs are easy to buy and sell, and they can be used to hedge against market volatility.

THE 6 ETFS YOU'LL NEED TO BECOME A MILLIONAIRE

If you want to become a millionaire, you'll need to invest in the right ETFs. Here are the six ETFs you'll need to get started:

1. Vanguard Total Stock Market ETF (VTI): This ETF provides exposure to the entire U.S. stock market, including large-cap, mid-cap, and small-cap stocks.
2. iShares Core S&P 500 ETF (IVV): This ETF provides exposure to the 500 largest U.S. companies.
3. Vanguard Total International Stock ETF (VXUS): This ETF provides exposure to stocks from developed and emerging markets outside the U.S.
4. iShares Core U.S. Aggregate Bond ETF (AGG): This ETF provides exposure to the U.S. investment-grade bond market.
5. SPDR Gold Shares ETF (GLD): This ETF provides exposure to gold, a safe-haven asset.
6. iShares Core MSCI Emerging Markets ETF (IEMG): This ETF provides exposure to stocks from emerging markets.

HOW TO INVEST IN ETFS

Investing in ETFs is easy. All you need to do is open a brokerage account and fund it with cash. Then you can buy and sell ETFs just like stocks. You can also use a robo-advisor to invest in ETFs. Robo-advisors are automated investment services that use algorithms to manage your investments.

RISKS OF INVESTING IN ETFS

Like any investment, ETFs come with risks. The most common risk is market risk, which is the risk that the value of your investments will go down due to market volatility. Additionally, ETFs are subject to management fees and other expenses, which can reduce your returns.

CONCLUSION

ETFs are a great way to diversify your portfolio and get exposure to a wide range of asset classes. With the right ETFs, you can become a millionaire. The six ETFs we've discussed in this article are a great place to start. Just remember to do your research and understand the risks before investing.

Q: What are ETFs?

A: ETFs are investment funds that are traded on stock exchanges. They are composed of a basket of securities, such as stocks, bonds, and commodities. ETFs are typically low-cost, diversified, and tax efficient.

Q: What are the benefits of investing in ETFs?

A: ETFs offer a number of benefits to investors. They are typically low-cost, diversified, and tax efficient. They also provide access to a wide range of asset classes, such as stocks, bonds, commodities, and currencies. Additionally,

ETFs are easy to buy and sell, and they can be used to hedge against market volatility.

Q: What are the six ETFs I need to become a millionaire?

A: The six ETFs you'll need to become a millionaire are Vanguard Total Stock Market ETF (VTI), iShares Core S&P 500 ETF (IVV), Vanguard Total International Stock ETF (VXUS), iShares Core U.S. Aggregate Bond ETF (AGG), SPDR Gold Shares ETF (GLD), and iShares Core MSCI Emerging Markets ETF (IEMG).

Q: How do I invest in ETFs?

A: Investing in ETFs is easy. All you need to do is open a brokerage account and fund it with cash. Then you can buy and sell ETFs just like stocks. You can also use a robo-advisor to invest in ETFs.

Q: What are the risks of investing in ETFs?

A: Like any investment, ETFs come with risks. The most common risk is market risk, which is the risk that the value of your investments will go down due to market volatility. Additionally, ETFs are subject to management fees and other expenses, which can reduce your returns.

THE STOCK MARKET

Welcome to the world of stock market investing! Investing in the stock market can be a great way to build wealth and secure your financial future. But it can also be a daunting prospect for those who are new to the game. That's why we've put together this guide to stock market investing for beginners. We'll cover the basics of stock market investing, including what stocks are, how to buy and sell them, and how to make money in the stock market. We'll also discuss the risks associated with stock market investing and provide some tips for getting started. So, let's get started!

WHAT IS THE STOCK MARKET?

The stock market is a collection of exchanges where stocks, bonds, and other securities are bought and sold. It is a global network of exchanges, with the largest being the New York Stock Exchange (NYSE) and the Nasdaq. The stock market is a place where investors can buy and sell shares of publicly traded companies. When investors buy shares of a company, they become part owners of that company.

HOW DOES THE STOCK MARKET WORK?

The stock market works by matching buyers and sellers of stocks. When an investor wants to buy a stock, they place an order with a broker. The broker then finds a seller who is willing to sell the stock at the price the buyer is willing to pay. The buyer and seller then enter into a contract, and the stock is transferred from the seller to the buyer.

The stock market is also driven by supply and demand. When there is more demand for a stock than there is supply, the price of the stock will go up. Conversely, when there is more supply than demand, the price of the stock will go down.

WHAT ARE THE BENEFITS OF INVESTING IN THE STOCK MARKET?

There are many benefits to investing in the stock market. One of the biggest benefits is the potential for long-term growth. Over time, stocks have historically outperformed other investments, such as bonds and cash. This means that if you invest in stocks for the long term, you have the potential to earn higher returns than you would with other investments.

Another benefit of investing in the stock market is that it can provide a source of income. Dividends are payments made to shareholders by companies when they make a profit. When you own stocks, you are entitled to receive dividends, which can provide a steady stream of income.

Finally, investing in the stock market can be a great way to diversify your portfolio. By investing in different types of stocks, you can reduce your risk and increase your chances of earning a return.

WHAT ARE THE RISKS OF INVESTING IN THE STOCK MARKET?

While there are many benefits to investing in the stock market, there are also risks. One of the biggest risks is that the stock market is volatile. This means that stock prices can go up and down quickly, and you could lose money if you invest in stocks.

Another risk is that you could be investing in a company that goes bankrupt. If a company goes bankrupt, you could lose all of your investment.

Finally, investing in the stock market requires a certain amount of knowledge and skill. If you don't have the necessary knowledge and skill, you could make bad decisions and lose money.

CONCLUSION

Investing in the stock market can be a great way to build wealth and secure your financial future. But it is important to understand the risks associated with stock market investing and to have the knowledge and skill necessary to make informed decisions. We hope this guide has provided you with a better understanding of the stock market and how to get started investing. Good luck!

Q: What is the stock market?

A: The stock market is a collection of exchanges where stocks, bonds, and other securities are bought and sold. It is a global network of exchanges, with the largest being the New York Stock Exchange (NYSE) and the Nasdaq.

Q: How does the stock market work?

A: The stock market works by matching buyers and sellers of stocks. When an investor wants to buy a stock, they place an order with a broker. The broker then finds a seller who is willing to sell the stock at the price the buyer is willing to pay. The buyer and seller then enter into a contract, and the stock is transferred from the seller to the buyer.

Q: What are the benefits of investing in the stock market?

A: There are many benefits to investing in the stock market. One of the biggest benefits is the potential for long-term growth. Over time, stocks have historically outperformed other investments, such as bonds and cash. This means that if you invest in stocks for the long term, you have the potential to earn higher returns than you would with other investments.

Q: What are the risks of investing in the stock market?

A: While there are many benefits to investing in the stock market, there are also risks. One of the biggest risks is that the stock market is volatile. This means that stock prices can go up and down quickly, and you could lose money if you invest in stocks. Another risk is that you could be investing in a company that goes bankrupt. If a company goes bankrupt, you could lose all of your investment.

Q: What knowledge and skill do I need to invest in the stock market?

A: Investing in the stock market requires a certain amount of knowledge and skill. You should have a basic understanding of how the stock market works and be familiar with different types of stocks and investments. You should also have a good understanding of financial concepts such as risk and return. Finally, you should have the ability to make informed decisions and manage your investments.

FIVE UNIQUE INVESTMENTS THAT AREN'T STOCKS

Investing in stocks is a great way to build wealth over time, but it's not the only way. There are many other types of investments that can help you diversify your portfolio and potentially increase your returns. Here are five unique investments that aren't stocks.

REAL ESTATE

Real estate is one of the most popular investments for those looking to diversify their portfolios. Investing in real estate can be a great way to generate passive income and build wealth over time. Real estate investments can range from buying a rental property to investing in a real estate investment trust (REIT).

BONDS

Bonds are another popular investment option for those looking to diversify their portfolios. Bonds are essentially loans that are made to governments or corporations. When you invest in bonds, you are essentially lending money to the issuer in exchange for a fixed rate of return. Bonds are generally considered to be a low-risk investment, but they can also provide a steady stream of income.

COMMODITIES

Commodities are physical goods such as oil, gold, and wheat that are traded on the commodities market. Investing in commodities can be a great way to diversify your portfolio and potentially increase your returns. Commodities can be volatile, so it's important to do your research before investing.

CRYPTOCURRENCY

Cryptocurrency is a digital currency that is not backed by any government or central bank. Cryptocurrency is becoming increasingly popular as an investment option due to its potential for high returns. Cryptocurrency is a highly volatile investment, so it's important to do your research before investing.

ALTERNATIVE INVESTMENTS

Alternative investments are investments that are not stocks, bonds, or commodities. Examples of alternative investments include venture capital, private equity, and hedge funds. Alternative investments can be risky, so it's important to do your research before investing.

CONCLUSION

Investing in stocks is a great way to build wealth over time, but it's not the only way. There are many other types of investments that can help you diversify your portfolio and potentially increase your returns. Real estate, bonds, commodities, cryptocurrency, and alternative investments are all unique investments that can help you diversify your portfolio and potentially increase your returns. However, it's important to do your research before investing in any of these investments, as they can be risky.

Q: What are alternative investments?

A: Alternative investments are investments that are not stocks, bonds, or commodities. Examples of alternative investments include venture capital, private equity, and hedge funds.

Q: What is cryptocurrency?

A: Cryptocurrency is a digital currency that is not backed by any government or central bank. Cryptocurrency is becoming increasingly popular as an investment option due to its potential for high returns.

Q: What is a bond?

A: Bonds are essentially loans that are made to governments or corporations. When you invest in bonds, you are essentially lending money to the issuer in exchange for a fixed rate of return.

Q: What is a REIT?

A: A REIT (Real Estate Investment Trust) is a type of investment vehicle that allows investors to invest in real estate without having to purchase and manage physical properties.

Q: What is the risk associated with investing in commodities?

A: Investing in commodities can be risky, as the prices of commodities can be volatile. It's important to do your research before investing in commodities.

6 STOCKS TO BUY AND HOLD

Investing in stocks can be a great way to build wealth over time. But with so many stocks to choose from, it can be difficult to know which ones to buy and hold. In this article, we'll look at six stocks that are worth considering for long-term investments. We'll discuss their potential for growth, their current performance, and their risk factors. By the end of this article, you'll have a better understanding of which stocks to buy and hold for the long term.

WHAT ARE STOCKS?

Stocks are a type of security that represents ownership in a company. When you buy a stock, you become a part-owner of the company and are entitled to a portion of its profits. Stocks can be bought and sold on the stock market, and their prices can fluctuate based on a variety of factors.

WHAT ARE THE BENEFITS OF INVESTING IN STOCKS?

Investing in stocks can be a great way to build wealth over time. Stocks have the potential to generate higher returns than other investments, such as bonds or cash. They also offer diversification, which can help reduce risk. Additionally, stocks can provide a steady stream of income in the form of dividends.

WHAT ARE THE RISKS OF INVESTING IN STOCKS?

Investing in stocks carries some risk. The stock market can be volatile, and stock prices can go up and down quickly. Additionally, stocks can be affected by a variety of factors, such as economic conditions, political events, and company performance. It's important to understand the risks before investing in stocks.

6 STOCKS TO BUY AND HOLD

Now that we've discussed the basics of stocks and the risks associated with investing in them, let's look at six stocks that are worth considering for long-term investments.

- Apple (AAPL): Apple is one of the world's largest technology companies and is known for its innovative products, such as the iPhone and iPad. The company has a strong track record of growth and is well positioned to benefit from the increasing demand for mobile devices.
- Amazon (AMZN): Amazon is one of the world's largest online retailers and is a leader in the e-commerce space. The company has a strong track record of growth and is well-positioned to benefit from the increasing demand for online shopping.
- Microsoft (MSFT): Microsoft is one of the world's largest software companies and is known for its Windows operating system and Office suite of products. The company has a strong track record of growth and is well positioned to benefit from the increasing demand for cloud computing services.
- Alphabet (GOOGL): Alphabet is the parent company of Google and is one of the world's largest technology

companies. The company has a strong track record of growth and is well positioned to benefit from the increasing demand for digital advertising.

- Berkshire Hathaway (BRK.B): Berkshire Hathaway is a holding company that owns a variety of businesses, including insurance, railroads, and energy. The company has a strong track record of growth and is well positioned to benefit from the increasing demand for its products and services.
- JPMorgan Chase (JPM): JPMorgan Chase is one of the world's largest banks and is known for its investment banking and asset management services. The company has a strong track record of growth and is well positioned to benefit from the increasing demand for financial services.

CONCLUSION

Investing in stocks can be a great way to build wealth over time. But with so many stocks to choose from, it can be difficult to know which ones to buy and hold. In this article, we've looked at six stocks that are worth considering for long-term investments. We've discussed their potential for growth, their current performance, and their risk factors. By understanding the basics of stocks and the risks associated with investing in them, you can make an informed decision about which stocks to buy and hold for the long term.

Q: What are stocks?

A: Stocks are a type of security that represents ownership in a company. When you buy a stock, you become a part-owner of the company and are entitled to a portion of its profits. Stocks can be bought and sold on the stock market, and their prices can fluctuate based on a variety of factors.

Q: What are the benefits of investing in stocks?

A: Investing in stocks can be a great way to build wealth over time. Stocks have the potential to generate higher returns than other investments, such as bonds or cash. They also offer diversification, which can help reduce risk. Additionally, stocks can provide a steady stream of income in the form of dividends.

Q: What are the risks of investing in stocks?

A: Investing in stocks carries some risk. The stock market can be volatile, and stock prices can go up and down quickly. Additionally, stocks can be affected by a variety of factors, such as economic conditions, political events, and company performance. It's important to understand the risks before investing in stocks.

Q: What stocks should I buy and hold?

A: The stocks you should buy, and hold will depend on your individual investment goals and risk tolerance. It's important to do your own research and understand the risks associated with each stock before investing. In this article, we've looked at six stocks that are worth considering for long-term investments.

Q: How do I buy stocks?

A: You can buy stocks through a broker or online trading platform. It's important to do your own research and understand the risks associated with each stock before investing. Additionally, it's important to understand the fees associated with buying and selling stocks.

INDEX FUNDS VS MUTUAL FUNDS: WHICH IS THE BEST INVESTMENT OPTION?

Investing in the stock market can be a great way to grow your wealth over time. But with so many different types of investments available, it can be difficult to decide which one is right for you. Two of the most popular types of investments are index funds and mutual funds. Both have their advantages and disadvantages, so it's important to understand the differences between them before making a decision.

WHAT ARE INDEX FUNDS?

Index funds are a type of mutual fund that tracks a specific stock market index, such as the S&P 500 or the Dow Jones Industrial Average. They are designed to provide investors with a low-cost way to invest in a broad range of stocks. Index funds are passively managed, meaning that they are not actively managed by a fund manager. Instead, they are designed to track the performance of the index they are based on.

ADVANTAGES OF INDEX FUNDS

Index funds offer a number of advantages for investors. First, they are typically much less expensive than actively managed mutual funds. This is because they do not require a fund manager to actively manage the fund, which can be a costly endeavor. Additionally, index funds are typically more diversified than actively managed funds, meaning that they are less likely to suffer from large losses due to a single stock or sector. Finally, index funds are often more tax-efficient than actively managed funds, as they are not subject to the same capital gains taxes.

DISADVANTAGES OF INDEX FUNDS

While index funds offer a number of advantages, they also have some drawbacks. First, they are not actively managed, meaning that they may not be able to take advantage of market opportunities that an actively managed fund could. Additionally, index funds may not be able to outperform the market, as they are designed to simply track the performance of the index they are based on. Finally, index funds may not be suitable for investors who are looking for more aggressive investments, as they are typically more conservative in nature.

WHAT ARE MUTUAL FUNDS?

Mutual funds are a type of investment that pools money from multiple investors and invests it in a variety of stocks, bonds, and other securities. Mutual funds are actively managed by a fund manager, who is responsible for selecting the investments and managing the fund's performance. Mutual funds are typically more expensive than index funds, as they require a fund manager to actively manage the fund.

ADVANTAGES OF MUTUAL FUNDS

Mutual funds offer a number of advantages for investors. First, they are actively managed, meaning that they can take advantage of market opportunities that an index fund may not be able to. Additionally, mutual funds can be more tax-efficient than index funds, as they are not subject to the same capital gains taxes. Finally, mutual funds can be more aggressive than index funds, as they are actively managed and can take advantage of more aggressive investments.

DISADVANTAGES OF MUTUAL FUNDS

While mutual funds offer a number of advantages, they also have some drawbacks. First, they are typically more expensive than index funds, as they require a fund manager to actively manage the fund. Additionally, mutual funds may not be able to outperform the market, as they are actively managed and may not be able to take advantage of market opportunities. Finally, mutual funds may not be suitable for investors who are looking for more conservative investments, as they are typically more aggressive in nature.

CONCLUSION

Index funds and mutual funds are both popular types of investments, and each has its own advantages and disadvantages. Index funds are typically less expensive and more tax-efficient than mutual funds, but they are not actively managed and may not be able to take advantage of market opportunities. Mutual funds are actively managed and can be more aggressive than index funds, but they are typically more expensive and may not be able to outperform the market. Ultimately, the best investment option for you will depend on your individual goals and risk tolerance.

Q: What is the difference between index funds and mutual funds?

A: The main difference between index funds and mutual funds is that index funds are passively managed, meaning that they are not actively managed by a fund manager. Mutual funds, on the other hand, are actively managed by a fund manager. Additionally, index funds are typically less expensive and more tax-efficient than mutual funds, but they may not be able to take advantage of market opportunities. Mutual funds are typically more expensive and may not be able to outperform the market, but they can be more aggressive than index funds.

Q: What are the advantages of index funds?

A: Index funds offer a number of advantages for investors. First, they are typically much less expensive than actively managed mutual funds. Additionally, index funds are typically more diversified than actively managed funds, meaning that they are less likely to suffer from large losses due to a single stock or sector. Finally, index funds are often more tax-efficient than actively managed funds, as they are not subject to the same capital gains taxes.

Q: What are the advantages of mutual funds?

A: Mutual funds offer a number of advantages for investors. First, they are actively managed, meaning that they can take advantage of market opportunities that an index fund may not be able to. Additionally, mutual funds can be more tax-efficient than index funds, as they are not subject to the same capital gains taxes. Finally, mutual funds can be more aggressive than index funds, as they are actively managed and can take advantage of more aggressive investments.

Q: Which type of investment is best for me?

A: The best investment option for you will depend on your individual goals and risk tolerance. Index funds are typically less expensive and more tax-efficient than mutual funds, but they are not actively managed and may not be able to take advantage of market opportunities. Mutual funds are actively managed and can be more aggressive than index funds, but they are typically more expensive and may not be able to outperform the market. Ultimately, it is important to consider your individual goals and risk tolerance when deciding which type of investment is best for you.

Q: What is the difference between index funds and ETFs?

A: The main difference between index funds and ETFs (Exchange Traded Funds) is that index funds are passively managed, meaning that they are not actively managed by a fund manager. ETFs, on the other hand, are actively managed by a fund manager. Additionally, index funds are typically less expensive and more tax-efficient than ETFs, but they may not be able to take advantage of market opportunities. ETFs are typically more expensive and may not be able to outperform the market, but they can be more aggressive than index funds.

STOCK MARKET FOR BEGINNERS

Welcome to the world of stock market investing! Investing in the stock market can be a great way to build wealth and secure your financial future. But it can also be a daunting prospect for those who are new to the game. That's why we've put together this guide to stock market investing for beginners. We'll cover the basics of stock market investing, including what stocks are, how to buy and sell them, and how to make money in the stock market. We'll also discuss the risks associated with stock market investing and provide some tips for getting started. So, let's get started!

WHAT IS THE STOCK MARKET?

The stock market is a collection of exchanges where stocks, bonds, and other securities are bought and sold. It is a global network of exchanges, with the largest being the New York Stock Exchange (NYSE) and the Nasdaq. The stock market is a place where investors can buy and sell shares of publicly traded companies. When investors buy shares of a company, they become part owners of that company.

HOW DOES THE STOCK MARKET WORK?

The stock market works by matching buyers and sellers of stocks. When an investor wants to buy a stock, they place an order with a broker. The broker then finds a seller who is willing to sell the stock at the price the buyer is willing to pay. The buyer and seller then enter into a contract, and the stock is transferred from the seller to the buyer.

The stock market is also driven by supply and demand. When there is more demand for a stock than there is supply, the price of the stock will go up. Conversely, when there is more supply than demand, the price of the stock will go down.

WHAT ARE THE BENEFITS OF INVESTING IN THE STOCK MARKET?

There are many benefits to investing in the stock market. One of the biggest benefits is the potential for long-term growth. Over time, stocks have historically outperformed other investments, such as bonds and cash. This means that if you invest in stocks for the long term, you have the potential to earn higher returns than you would with other investments.

Another benefit of investing in the stock market is that it can provide a source of income. Dividends are payments made to shareholders by companies when they make a profit. When you own stocks, you are entitled to receive dividends, which can provide a steady stream of income.

Finally, investing in the stock market can be a great way to diversify your portfolio. By investing in different types of stocks, you can reduce your risk and increase your chances of earning a return.

WHAT ARE THE RISKS OF INVESTING IN THE STOCK MARKET?

While there are many benefits to investing in the stock market, there are also risks. One of the biggest risks is that the stock market is volatile. This means that stock prices can go up and down quickly, and you could lose money if you invest in stocks.

Another risk is that you could be investing in a company that goes bankrupt. If a company goes bankrupt, you could lose all of your investment.

Finally, investing in the stock market requires a certain amount of knowledge and skill. If you don't have the necessary knowledge and skill, you could make bad decisions and lose money.

CONCLUSION

Investing in the stock market can be a great way to build wealth and secure your financial future. But it is important to understand the risks associated with stock market investing and to have the knowledge and skill necessary to make informed decisions. We hope this guide has provided you with a better understanding of the stock market and how to get started investing. Good luck!

Q: What is the stock market?

A: The stock market is a collection of exchanges where stocks, bonds, and other securities are bought and sold. It is a global network of exchanges, with the largest being the New York Stock Exchange (NYSE) and the Nasdaq.

Q: How does the stock market work?

A: The stock market works by matching buyers and sellers of stocks. When an investor wants to buy a stock, they place an order with a broker. The broker then finds a seller who is willing to sell the stock at the price the buyer is willing to pay. The buyer and seller then enter into a contract, and the stock is transferred from the seller to the buyer.

Q: What are the benefits of investing in the stock market?

A: There are many benefits to investing in the stock market. One of the biggest benefits is the potential for long-term growth. Over time, stocks have historically outperformed other investments, such as bonds and cash. This means that if you invest in stocks for the long term, you have the potential to earn higher returns than you would with other investments.

Q: What are the risks of investing in the stock market?

A: While there are many benefits to investing in the stock market, there are also risks. One of the biggest risks is that the stock market is volatile. This means that stock prices can go up and down quickly, and you could lose money if you invest in stocks. Another risk is that you could be investing in a company that goes bankrupt. If a company goes bankrupt, you could lose all of your investment.

Q: What knowledge and skill do I need to invest in the stock market?

A: Investing in the stock market requires a certain amount of knowledge and skill. You should have a basic understanding of how the stock market works and be familiar with different types of stocks and investments. You should also have a good understanding of financial concepts such as risk and return. Finally, you should have the ability to make informed decisions and manage your investments.

TOP FIVE INDEX FUNDS

Investing in index funds is a great way to diversify your portfolio and reduce your risk. Index funds are a type of mutual fund that tracks a specific market index, such as the S&P 500 or the Dow Jones Industrial Average. By investing in an index fund, you are essentially investing in the entire market, rather than just a few individual stocks. This means that you are less likely to suffer from the volatility of individual stocks, and you can benefit from the overall performance of the market.

Index funds are a great way to get started with investing, as they are relatively low-cost and easy to manage. They are also a great way to diversify your portfolio, as they provide exposure to a wide range of stocks and bonds. In this article, we will take a look at the top five index funds that you should consider investing in.

WHAT IS AN INDEX FUND?

An index fund is a type of mutual fund that tracks a specific market index, such as the S&P 500 or the Dow Jones Industrial Average. Index funds are designed to provide investors with exposure to a wide range of stocks and bonds, without having to pick individual stocks. By investing in an index fund, you are essentially investing in the entire market, rather than just a few individual stocks. This means that you are less likely to suffer from the volatility of individual stocks, and you can benefit from the overall performance of the market.

BENEFITS OF INVESTING IN INDEX FUNDS

Index funds offer a number of benefits to investors. They are relatively low-cost and easy to manage, making them a great option for those just getting started with investing. They also provide diversification, as they provide exposure to a wide range of stocks and bonds. Additionally, index funds are generally less volatile than individual stocks, meaning that you are less likely to suffer from large losses.

TOP FIVE INDEX FUNDS

There are a number of index funds available to investors, but here are the top five that you should consider investing in:

1. Vanguard Total Stock Market Index Fund (VTSMX): This fund tracks the performance of the entire U.S. stock market, providing investors with exposure to a wide range of stocks.
2. Vanguard Total International Stock Index Fund (VGTSX): This fund tracks the performance of the entire international stock market, providing investors with exposure to a wide range of stocks from around the world.
3. Vanguard Total Bond Market Index Fund (VBMFX): This fund tracks the performance of the entire U.S. bond market, providing investors with exposure to a wide range of bonds.
4. Vanguard Total International Bond Index Fund (VTABX): This fund tracks the performance of the entire

international bond market, providing investors with exposure to a wide range of bonds from around the world.

5. Vanguard Total World Stock Index Fund (VTWSX): This fund tracks the performance of the entire global stock market, providing investors with exposure to a wide range of stocks from around the world.

HOW TO CHOOSE THE RIGHT INDEX FUND

When choosing an index fund, it is important to consider your investment goals and risk tolerance. You should also consider the fees associated with the fund, as well as the performance of the fund over time. Additionally, you should consider the type of index that the fund tracks, as some funds may track different indices.

CONCLUSION

Index funds are a great way to get started with investing, as they are relatively low-cost and easy to manage. They are also a great way to diversify your portfolio, as they provide exposure to a wide range of stocks and bonds. In this article, we have looked at the top five index funds that you should consider investing in. When choosing an index fund, it is important to consider your investment goals and risk tolerance, as well as the fees associated with the fund and the performance of the fund over time.

Q: What is an index fund?

A: An index fund is a type of mutual fund that tracks a specific market index, such as the S&P 500 or the Dow Jones Industrial Average. Index funds are designed to provide investors with exposure to a wide range of stocks and bonds, without having to pick individual stocks.

Q: What are the benefits of investing in index funds?

A: Index funds offer a number of benefits to investors. They are relatively low-cost and easy to manage, making them a great option for those just getting started with investing. They also provide diversification, as they provide exposure to a wide range of stocks and bonds. Additionally, index funds are generally less volatile than individual stocks, meaning that you are less likely to suffer from large losses.

Q: What are the top five index funds that I should consider investing in?

A: The top five index funds that you should consider investing in are the Vanguard Total Stock Market Index Fund (VTSMX), the Vanguard Total International Stock Index Fund (VGTSX), the Vanguard Total Bond Market Index Fund (VBMFX), the Vanguard Total International Bond Index Fund (VTABX), and the Vanguard Total World Stock Index Fund (VTWSX).

Q: How do I choose the right index fund?

A: When choosing an index fund, it is important to consider your investment goals and risk tolerance. You should also consider the fees associated with the fund, as well as the performance of the fund over time. Additionally, you should consider the type of index that the fund tracks, as some funds may track different indices.

Q: Is investing in index funds a good way to diversify my portfolio?

A: Yes, investing in index funds is a great way to diversify your portfolio and reduce your risk. Index funds provide exposure to a wide range of stocks and bonds, without having to pick individual stocks. This means that you are less likely to suffer from the volatility of individual stocks, and you can benefit from the overall performance of the market.

THE POWER OF A MEANINGFUL RELATIONSHIP

John and Sarah had been married for five years, but their relationship had been strained for some time. They had grown apart, and it seemed like they were just going through the motions of being married. They had both been so busy with their careers that they had neglected their relationship, and it was starting to show.

John and Sarah had been together since college, and they had always been very close. They had shared a lot of great memories and had a lot of fun together. But as time went on, they had both become more focused on their careers and less focused on each other.

John had been working long hours at his job, and Sarah had been working hard to get her business off the ground. They had both been so busy that they had neglected their relationship, and it was starting to show.

One day, John and Sarah decided to take a break from their busy lives and go on a weekend getaway. They decided to go to a cabin in the woods, far away from the hustle and bustle of the city.

When they arrived at the cabin, they were both surprised to find that it was much more beautiful than they had expected. The cabin was nestled in a lush forest, and the air was filled with the scent of pine trees.

John and Sarah spent the weekend exploring the area and enjoying each other's company. They talked about their lives and their dreams, and they reconnected in a way that they hadn't in a long time.

When they returned home, they both felt refreshed and energized.

HOW TO MANAGE DEBT

Debt can be a tricky thing to manage. It can be overwhelming and stressful, but it doesn't have to be. With the right strategies and a little bit of discipline, you can manage your debt and even pay it off.

The first step to managing your debt is to understand it. Take a look at all of your debts and make a list of them. Include the amount of each debt, the interest rate, and the minimum payment. This will give you a better understanding of your financial situation and help you create a plan to pay off your debt.

Once you have a list of your debts, you can start to create a plan to pay them off. Start by making a budget. Figure out how much money you have coming in each month and how much you need to spend on necessities like rent, food, and utilities. Then, figure out how much money you have left over each month to put towards your debt.

Once you have a budget in place, you can start to make payments on your debt. Start by making the minimum payments on all of your debts. This will help you avoid late fees and keep your credit score in good standing.

If you have extra money left over each month, you can start to make larger payments on your debt. Start by paying off the debt with the highest interest rate first. This will save you money in the long run because you'll be paying less interest.

You can also consider consolidating your debt. This means taking out a loan to pay off all of your debts. This can be a good option if you have a lot of debt and you're having trouble making payments. Just make sure to shop around for the best interest rate and terms.

Finally, make sure to stay disciplined. It can be tempting to spend money on things you don't need, but it's important to stay focused on your goal of paying off your debt. Make sure to stick to your budget and make payments on time.

Managing debt can be overwhelming, but it doesn't have to be. With the right strategies and a little bit of discipline, you can manage your debt and even pay it off. Start by understanding your debt, creating a budget, and making payments on time. With a little bit of effort, you can be debt-free in no time.

HOW TO DEAL WITH FAILURE

It was a cold winter morning and the sun had just begun to rise. The sky was a deep blue, and the snow was still fresh on the ground. I was walking down the street, my head hung low, my heart heavy with the weight of failure. I had just failed my final exam, and I was feeling defeated.

I had worked so hard for this exam, and I had been so sure that I would pass. But I had failed, and I was feeling like a complete failure. I had let myself down, and I was feeling like I had let everyone else down too.

I kept walking, my head still hung low, my heart still heavy with the weight of failure. I was so lost in my thoughts that I didn't even notice the old man walking towards me. He was an elderly man, with a kind face and a gentle smile. He stopped in front of me and said, "You look like you could use a friend."

I looked up at him, and I could feel the tears welling up in my eyes. I tried to hold them back, but they started to fall. The old man reached out and put his hand on my shoulder. He said, "It's okay to cry. It's okay to feel sad. But it's also okay to pick yourself up and try again."

I looked up at him, and I could feel the weight of failure lifting from my shoulders. I knew he was right. I had failed, but that didn't mean I was a failure. I could still try again. I could still learn from my mistakes and do better next time.

The old man smiled at me and said, "Failure is part of life. It's how we learn and grow. Don't let it stop you from trying again. Don't let it stop you from reaching your goals."

I nodded, and I could feel the tears drying on my cheeks. I thanked the old man for his words of wisdom, and I watched him walk away. I took a deep breath and looked up at the sky. I knew what I had to do.

I had to pick myself up and try again. I had to learn from my mistakes and do better next time. I had to keep going, no matter how hard it was. I had to keep pushing forward, no matter how many times I failed.

I started walking again, my head held high, my heart no longer heavy with the weight of failure. I knew that I could do it. I knew that I could reach my goals, no matter how many times I failed. I knew that I could learn from my mistakes and do better next time.

I kept walking, and I kept pushing forward. I kept trying, and I kept learning. I kept growing, and I kept reaching my goals. I kept dealing with failure, and I kept succeeding.

HOW TO COMMUNICATE EFFECTIVELY

Communication is an essential part of life. It is the way we interact with others, express our thoughts and feelings, and build relationships. Effective communication is the key to success in any endeavor, whether it be personal or professional.

John and Sarah had been married for five years and were struggling to communicate effectively. They had been through a lot together, but their communication had become strained, and they were having difficulty understanding each other.

One day, John and Sarah decided to take a break from their everyday lives and go on a camping trip. They packed up their tent and supplies and headed out into the wilderness.

Once they arrived at their campsite, they set up their tent and began to explore the area. As they walked, they talked about their lives and their struggles with communication. They discussed how they had been unable to express their feelings and how they had been unable to understand each other.

John and Sarah decided to take a break from their conversation and enjoy the beauty of nature. They sat by a lake and watched the sun set. As they watched the sun set, they talked about how they could improve their communication.

John suggested that they start by listening to each other. He said that it was important to really hear what the other person was saying and to try to understand their point of view. Sarah agreed and said that it was also important to be honest and open with each other.

John and Sarah decided to practice what they had discussed. They began to talk about their feelings and their thoughts. They listened to each other and tried to understand each other's point of view. They talked about their hopes and dreams and their fears and worries.

As they talked, they began to understand each other better. They began to see each other's perspective and to appreciate each other's feelings. They began to communicate more effectively, and their relationship began to improve.

John and Sarah continued to practice their communication skills on their camping trip. They talked about their lives and their struggles, and they listened to each other. They began to understand each other better and their relationship began to grow stronger.

When they returned home, John and Sarah continued to practice their communication skills. They continued to listen to each other and to understand each other's point of view. They continued to be honest and open with each other and their relationship continued to improve.

John and Sarah's story is a great example of how effective communication can improve relationships. By listening to each other and trying to understand each other's point of view, they were able to improve their communication and their relationship.

Effective communication is essential for any relationship. It is the key to understanding each other and building strong relationships. By listening to each other and being honest and open with each other, we can improve our communication and our relationships.

LOGIC AND REASONING

The sun was setting on the horizon, painting the sky in a beautiful array of colors. The birds were singing their evening songs, and the wind was blowing gently through the trees. It was a peaceful evening, and the perfect time for contemplation.

John was sitting on a bench in the park, watching the sunset and thinking about the world around him. He was a man of logic and reason, and he was always trying to make sense of the world. He had a deep curiosity about the way things worked, and he was always looking for answers.

John had been studying philosophy for many years, and he had come to the conclusion that the only way to truly understand the world was through logic and reason. He believed that if he could understand the logic behind the world, he could make sense of it.

John had been trying to figure out the logic behind the universe for some time now, but he had yet to find any answers. He was beginning to feel frustrated, and he was starting to doubt his own beliefs. He was starting to think that maybe he was wrong, and that the world was too complex for him to understand.

Just then, a voice interrupted his thoughts.

"Excuse me, sir," the voice said. "I couldn't help but notice that you seem to be in deep thought. Is there something I can help you with?"

John looked up to see a young man standing in front of him. He was wearing a white robe and had a kind face.

"Yes," John said. "I'm trying to figure out the logic behind the universe, but I'm having trouble. Do you have any advice?"

The young man smiled. "Yes, I do," he said. "The key to understanding the universe is to look at it from a logical perspective. You must use your reason and your logic to make sense of the world. Once you understand the logic behind the universe, you will be able to make sense of it."

John nodded. He had heard this advice before, but he had never really taken it to heart. He thanked the young man and asked him his name.

"My name is Socrates," the young man said. "I'm a philosopher, and I believe that the only way to truly understand the world is through logic and reason."

John thanked Socrates for his advice and the two men parted ways. John went home and began to think about what Socrates had said. He realized that he had been looking at the world in the wrong way. He had been trying to make sense of it without using logic and reason.

John began to study philosophy more deeply, and he soon realized that Socrates was right. He began to understand the logic behind the universe, and he was able to make sense of it. He was able to see the beauty and the complexity of the world, and he was able to appreciate it in a way he had never been able to before.

John had found the answers he was looking for, and he was grateful to Socrates for his advice. He had learned that the only way to truly understand the world was through logic and reason. He had learned that if he used his logic and reason, he could make sense of the world and appreciate its beauty.

HOW TO HANDLE OUR EMOTIONS

We all experience emotions in our lives, and it's important to learn how to handle them. Emotions can be powerful and overwhelming, and if we don't know how to manage them, they can lead to destructive behavior. Learning how to handle our emotions is an important part of life, and it can help us to lead healthier and happier lives.

The first step in learning how to handle our emotions is to recognize them. We all experience a wide range of emotions, from joy and excitement to sadness and anger. It's important to be aware of what we're feeling and to take the time to identify the emotion. This can help us to better understand our feelings and to take the necessary steps to manage them.

Once we've identified our emotions, it's important to take a step back and assess the situation. We should ask ourselves why we're feeling the way we do and what we can do to address the issue. This can help us to gain perspective and to make better decisions.

The next step is to take action. We should take the time to think about how we can best handle our emotions. This could involve talking to someone, writing down our thoughts, or engaging in a physical activity. Taking action can help us to process our emotions and to move forward.

It's also important to practice self-care. Taking care of ourselves is essential for managing our emotions. This could involve getting enough sleep, eating healthily, and engaging in activities that bring us joy. Taking care of ourselves can help us to better manage our emotions and to lead healthier lives.

Finally, it's important to remember that our emotions are valid. We all experience a wide range of emotions, and it's important to recognize that they are all valid. We should take the time to acknowledge our feelings and to accept them. This can help us to better manage our emotions and to lead healthier lives.

Learning how to handle our emotions is an important part of life. It can help us to lead healthier and happier lives. We should take the time to recognize our emotions, assess the situation, take action, practice self-care, and remember that our emotions are valid. Taking these steps can help us to better manage our emotions and to lead healthier lives.

Once upon a time, there was a small village in the middle of nowhere. The village was filled with people who were content with their lives and rarely had any problems.

One day, however, a strange thing happened. A mysterious stranger appeared in the village and began to cause all sorts of problems. He would cause arguments between people, start fights, and generally make life difficult for everyone.

The villagers were at a loss as to what to do. They had never encountered such a problem before and had no idea how to solve it. They tried to talk to the stranger, but he refused to listen. They tried to ignore him, but he kept causing trouble.

Finally, the villagers decided to come together and try to solve the problem. They gathered in the village square and discussed the situation. After much debate, they decided that the best way to solve the problem was to come up with a plan.

The plan was simple. They would all work together to find a way to get rid of the stranger. They would use their collective knowledge and skills to come up with a solution.

The villagers worked hard and eventually came up with a plan. They decided to build a giant wall around the village. This would keep the stranger out and protect the villagers from any further trouble.

The villagers worked together to build the wall. It took them several weeks, but eventually they finished it. The wall was strong and sturdy, and the villagers were relieved to know that they were safe from the stranger.

The villagers celebrated their success and thanked each other for their hard work. They had come together and solved a problem that seemed impossible.

From then on, the villagers were more aware of the problems that could arise in their village. Whenever a problem arose, they would come together and work together to find a solution.

The villagers had learned an important lesson: that by working together, they could solve any problem. They had learned the power of problem solving and it would serve them well in the future.

The villagers lived happily ever after, safe in the knowledge that they could solve any problem that came their way.

PROBLEM SOLVING: A COMPREHENSIVE GUIDE

Problem solving is an essential skill for success in life. It is the ability to identify and solve problems in a timely and efficient manner. Problem solving involves a range of cognitive skills, including critical thinking, analysis, and creative thinking. It is a process that requires patience, practice, and perseverance. This guide will provide an overview of problem solving, including the different types of problem solving, the steps involved in problem solving, and strategies for successful problem solving.

WHAT IS PROBLEM SOLVING?

Problem solving is the process of identifying and solving problems. It involves the use of cognitive skills such as critical thinking, analysis, and creative thinking. Problem solving is a process that requires patience, practice, and perseverance. It is a skill that can be developed and improved with practice.

TYPES OF PROBLEM SOLVING

There are several different types of problem solving. These include analytical problem solving, creative problem solving, and systems thinking.

ANALYTICAL PROBLEM SOLVING

Analytical problem solving involves the use of logical reasoning and data analysis to identify and solve problems. It involves the use of deductive reasoning to identify the root cause of a problem and then develop a solution.

CREATIVE PROBLEM SOLVING

Creative problem solving involves the use of creative thinking to identify and solve problems. It involves the use of brainstorming, lateral thinking, and other creative techniques to generate new ideas and solutions.

SYSTEMS THINKING

Systems thinking is a type of problem solving that involves the use of systems thinking to identify and solve problems. It involves the use of systems thinking to identify the root cause of a problem and then develop a solution.

STEPS IN PROBLEM SOLVING

Problem solving is a process that involves several steps. These steps include:

1. Identifying the Problem: The first step in problem solving is to identify the problem. This involves understanding the problem and its root cause.
2. Analyzing the Problem: The second step in problem solving is to analyze the problem. This involves gathering information and data about the problem and analyzing it to identify potential solutions.

3. Developing Solutions: The third step in problem solving is to develop solutions. This involves brainstorming potential solutions and evaluating them to determine the best solution.
4. Implementing Solutions: The fourth step in problem solving is to implement the solution. This involves taking action to implement the solution and monitoring the results.

STRATEGIES FOR SUCCESSFUL PROBLEM SOLVING

There are several strategies that can be used to improve problem solving skills. These include:

1. Developing Critical Thinking Skills: Developing critical thinking skills is essential for successful problem solving. Critical thinking involves the use of logic and reasoning to identify and solve problems.
2. Practicing Problem Solving: Practicing problem solving is an important way to improve problem solving skills. This involves practicing problem solving techniques and strategies in a variety of situations.
3. Working in Teams: Working in teams is an effective way to improve problem solving skills. Working in teams allows individuals to share ideas and brainstorm solutions to problems.
4. Taking Time to Reflect: Taking time to reflect on problems and solutions is an important part of problem solving. This involves taking time to think about the problem and potential solutions before taking action.

CONCLUSION

Problem solving is an essential skill for success in life. It involves the use of cognitive skills such as critical thinking, analysis, and creative thinking. Problem solving is a process that requires patience, practice, and perseverance. This guide has provided an overview of problem solving, including the different types of problem solving, the steps involved in problem solving, and strategies for successful problem solving.

Q: What is problem solving?

A: Problem solving is the process of identifying and solving problems. It involves the use of cognitive skills such as critical thinking, analysis, and creative thinking. Problem solving is a process that requires patience, practice, and perseverance.

Q: What are the different types of problem solving?

A: The different types of problem solving include analytical problem solving, creative problem solving, and systems thinking.

Q: What are the steps in problem solving?

A: The steps in problem solving include identifying the problem, analyzing the problem, developing solutions, and implementing solutions.

Q: What strategies can be used to improve problem solving skills?

A: Strategies that can be used to improve problem solving skills include developing critical thinking skills, practicing problem solving, working in teams, and taking time to reflect.

Q: How can problem solving be developed and improved?

A: Problem solving can be developed and improved with practice. It is important to practice problem solving techniques and strategies in a variety of situations. Working in teams is also an effective way to improve problem solving skills.

HOW TO BE RESILIENT

Resilience is a key factor in achieving success in life. It is the ability to bounce back from adversity and to keep going despite the challenges that life throws at us. Resilience is a skill that can be learned and developed, and it is essential for anyone who wants to reach their goals and live a fulfilling life. In this article, we will explore what resilience is, how to develop it, and how to use it to become successful.

WHAT IS RESILIENCE?

Resilience is the ability to cope with and adapt to difficult situations. It is the capacity to recover quickly from setbacks, to remain optimistic in the face of adversity, and to keep going despite the challenges that life throws at us. Resilience is a skill that can be learned and developed, and it is essential for anyone who wants to reach their goals and live a fulfilling life.

Resilience is not about being strong or tough; it is about being able to cope with difficult situations and to keep going despite the challenges. It is about having the courage to face adversity and to keep going despite the obstacles. It is about having the strength to keep going even when things seem impossible.

HOW TO DEVELOP RESILIENCE

Developing resilience is not something that happens overnight; it takes time and effort. Here are some tips for developing resilience:

1. Acknowledge Your Feelings: It is important to acknowledge your feelings and to accept them. Acknowledge that you are feeling overwhelmed, scared, or anxious, and accept that these feelings are normal.
2. Take Care of Yourself: Taking care of yourself is essential for developing resilience. Make sure to get enough sleep, eat healthy, and exercise regularly.
3. Develop a Support System: Having a strong support system is essential for developing resilience. Reach out to family and friends for support and seek professional help if needed.
4. Practice Self-Compassion: It is important to be kind to yourself and to practice self-compassion. Remind yourself that you are doing the best you can and that it is okay to make mistakes.
5. Develop a Positive Mindset: Developing a positive mindset is essential for developing resilience. Focus on the positive aspects of life and practice gratitude.
6. Take Action: Taking action is essential for developing resilience. Take small steps towards your goals and celebrate your successes.
7. Learn from Your Mistakes: It is important to learn from your mistakes and to use them as an opportunity to grow.

8. Find Meaning: Finding meaning in life is essential for developing resilience. Find something that gives your life purpose and meaning.
9. Practice Mindfulness: Practicing mindfulness is essential for developing resilience. Take time to be present in the moment and to focus on your breath.
10. Believe in Yourself: Believing in yourself is essential for developing resilience. Remind yourself that you are capable and that you can do anything you set your mind to.

CONCLUSION

Resilience is a key factor in achieving success in life. It is the ability to bounce back from adversity and to keep going despite the challenges that life throws at us. Resilience is a skill that can be learned and developed, and it is essential for anyone who wants to reach their goals and live a fulfilling life. By acknowledging your feelings, taking care of yourself, developing a support system, practicing self-compassion, developing a positive mindset, taking action, learning from your mistakes, finding meaning, practicing mindfulness, and believing in yourself, you can develop the resilience you need to reach your goals and live a fulfilling life.

Q: What is resilience?

A: Resilience is the ability to cope with and adapt to difficult situations. It is the capacity to recover quickly from setbacks, to remain optimistic in the face of adversity, and to keep going despite the challenges that life throws at us.

Q: How can I develop resilience?

A: You can develop resilience by acknowledging your feelings, taking care of yourself, developing a support system, practicing self-compassion, developing a positive mindset, taking action, learning from your mistakes, finding meaning, practicing mindfulness, and believing in yourself.

Q: What are the benefits of resilience?

A: The benefits of resilience include increased confidence, improved mental health, better problem-solving skills, increased creativity, and improved relationships.

Q: How can I stay resilient in difficult times?

A: To stay resilient in difficult times, it is important to take care of yourself, practice self-compassion, develop a positive mindset, take action, and believe in yourself.

Q: What is the difference between resilience and strength?

A: Resilience is the ability to cope with and adapt to difficult situations, while strength is the ability to withstand physical or mental pressure. Resilience is not about being strong or tough; it is about being able to cope with difficult situations and to keep going despite the challenges.

ANGER MANAGEMENT: HOW TO CONTROL YOUR EMOTIONS AND LIVE A HAPPIER LIFE

Anger is a normal emotion, but it can become a problem if it is not managed properly. Anger can lead to physical and emotional harm, and it can also damage relationships. Fortunately, there are ways to manage anger and live a happier life.

WHAT IS ANGER?

Anger is an emotion that is characterized by feelings of hostility, frustration, and aggression. It is a normal emotion, but it can become a problem if it is not managed properly. Anger can lead to physical and emotional harm, and it can also damage relationships.

WHAT CAUSES ANGER?

Anger can be caused by a variety of factors, including stress, frustration, fear, and even physical pain. It can also be caused by a person's beliefs or values, or by a perceived injustice.

HOW TO MANAGE ANGER

Managing anger can be difficult, but it is possible. Here are some tips for managing anger:

1. Identify the Cause: The first step in managing anger is to identify the cause. This can help you understand why you are feeling angry and can help you find ways to address the issue.
2. Take a Time Out: Taking a time out can help you calm down and gain perspective. It can also help you avoid saying or doing something you may regret later.
3. Talk to Someone: Talking to a friend, family member, or therapist can help you process your emotions and find ways to manage your anger.
4. Practice Relaxation Techniques: Relaxation techniques such as deep breathing, progressive muscle relaxation, and visualization can help you reduce stress and manage your anger.
5. Exercise: Exercise can help you reduce stress and release endorphins, which can help you feel better.
6. Get Enough Sleep: Getting enough sleep can help you manage your emotions and make better decisions.

WHEN TO SEEK PROFESSIONAL HELP

If you find that you are unable to manage your anger on your own, it may be time to seek professional help. A therapist can help you identify the causes of your anger and develop strategies for managing it.

CONCLUSION

Anger is a normal emotion, but it can become a problem if it is not managed properly. Fortunately, there are ways to manage anger and live a happier life. Identifying the cause of your anger, taking a time out, talking to someone, practicing relaxation techniques, exercising, and getting enough sleep can all help you manage your anger. If you find that you are unable to manage your anger on your own, it may be time to seek professional help.

Q: What is anger?

A: Anger is an emotion that is characterized by feelings of hostility, frustration, and aggression. It is a normal emotion, but it can become a problem if it is not managed properly.

Q: What causes anger?

A: Anger can be caused by a variety of factors, including stress, frustration, fear, and even physical pain. It can also be caused by a person's beliefs or values, or by a perceived injustice.

Q: How can I manage my anger?

A: Managing anger can be difficult, but it is possible. Identifying the cause of your anger, taking a time out, talking to someone, practicing relaxation techniques, exercising, and getting enough sleep can all help you manage your anger.

Q: When should I seek professional help for my anger?

A: If you find that you are unable to manage your anger on your own, it may be time to seek professional help. A therapist can help you identify the causes of your anger and develop strategies for managing it.

Q: What are some relaxation techniques I can use to manage my anger?

A: Relaxation techniques such as deep breathing, progressive muscle relaxation, and visualization can help you reduce stress and manage your anger.

ENTREPRENEURSHIP: THE PATH TO SUCCESS

Entrepreneurship is a journey that requires dedication, hard work, and a willingness to take risks. It is a path that can lead to great success, but it is not without its challenges. It is important to understand the basics of entrepreneurship and the different types of businesses that can be started. This article will provide an overview of entrepreneurship and the different types of businesses that can be started.

WHAT IS ENTREPRENEURSHIP?

Entrepreneurship is the process of starting and running a business. It involves identifying an opportunity, developing a business plan, and taking the necessary steps to launch and grow the business. Entrepreneurship is a journey that requires dedication, hard work, and a willingness to take risks. It is a path that can lead to great success, but it is not without its challenges.

TYPES OF BUSINESSES

There are many different types of businesses that can be started. Some of the most common types of businesses include:

- Sole Proprietorship: A sole proprietorship is a business owned and operated by one person. This type of business is relatively easy to set up and does not require any formal paperwork.
- Partnership: A partnership is a business owned and operated by two or more people. This type of business requires a formal agreement between the partners.
- Corporation: A corporation is a business owned by shareholders. This type of business requires formal paperwork and is subject to certain regulations.
- Limited Liability Company (LLC): An LLC is a business owned by members. This type of business provides limited liability protection to its members.
- Non-Profit: A non-profit is a business that is organized for a charitable or educational purpose. This type of business is exempt from certain taxes.

BENEFITS OF ENTREPRENEURSHIP

Entrepreneurship can provide many benefits, including:

- Financial Freedom: Starting a business can provide financial freedom and the potential for significant income.
- Flexibility: Entrepreneurs have the flexibility to set their own hours and work from anywhere.
- Independence: Entrepreneurs have the freedom to make their own decisions and be their own boss.
- Satisfaction: Entrepreneurs have the satisfaction of creating something from nothing and seeing it grow.

CHALLENGES OF ENTREPRENEURSHIP

Entrepreneurship can also present some challenges, including:

- Risk: Starting a business involves taking risks and there is no guarantee of success.
- Time: Starting a business can be time-consuming and require long hours.
- Money: Starting a business can require a significant amount of money.
- Stress: Running a business can be stressful and require a lot of hard work.

CONCLUSION

Entrepreneurship is a journey that requires dedication, hard work, and a willingness to take risks. It is a path that can lead to great success, but it is not without its challenges. It is important to understand the basics of entrepreneurship and the different types of businesses that can be started. With the right attitude and dedication, entrepreneurship can be a rewarding and fulfilling experience.

Q: What is entrepreneurship?

A: Entrepreneurship is the process of starting and running a business. It involves identifying an opportunity, developing a business plan, and taking the necessary steps to launch and grow the business.

Q: What are the benefits of entrepreneurship?

A: The benefits of entrepreneurship include financial freedom, flexibility, independence, and satisfaction.

Q: What are the challenges of entrepreneurship?

A: The challenges of entrepreneurship include risk, time, money, and stress.

Q: What types of businesses can be started?

A: The most common types of businesses that can be started include sole proprietorships, partnerships, corporations, limited liability companies (LLCs), and non-profits.

Q: Is entrepreneurship right for me?

A: Whether or not entrepreneurship is right for you depends on your goals, skills, and willingness to take risks. It is important to do your research and understand the basics of entrepreneurship before making a decision.

BASIC COMPUTER SKILLS

In today's digital world, having basic computer skills is essential for success. Whether you're a student, a professional, or a stay-at-home parent, having a basic understanding of computers and how to use them is a must. From basic word processing to more advanced tasks like coding and web design, having a good grasp of computer skills can open up a world of opportunities. In this article, we'll discuss the basics of computer skills and how to develop them.

WHAT ARE BASIC COMPUTER SKILLS?

Basic computer skills are the fundamental abilities and knowledge needed to use a computer. These skills include the ability to navigate a computer's operating system, use basic programs, and troubleshoot common problems. Basic computer skills are essential for anyone who wants to use a computer for work, school, or leisure.

WHAT ARE THE DIFFERENT TYPES OF COMPUTER SKILLS?

There are many different types of computer skills. Some of the most common include:

- Operating System Skills: This includes the ability to navigate a computer's operating system, such as Windows or Mac OS.

- Word Processing Skills: This includes the ability to create, edit, and format documents using a word processor, such as Microsoft Word.
- Spreadsheet Skills: This includes the ability to create, edit, and format spreadsheets using a spreadsheet program, such as Microsoft Excel.
- Database Skills: This includes the ability to create, edit, and format databases using a database program, such as Microsoft Access.
- Programming Skills: This includes the ability to write code using a programming language, such as HTML, CSS, or JavaScript.
- Web Design Skills: This includes the ability to create and design websites using HTML, CSS, and other web design tools.
- Networking Skills: This includes the ability to set up and maintain a computer network.
- Troubleshooting Skills: This includes the ability to diagnose and fix common computer problems.

HOW CAN I DEVELOP MY COMPUTER SKILLS?

Developing your computer skills is an ongoing process. Here are some tips to help you get started:

- Take a class: Taking a class is a great way to learn the basics of computer skills. Many community colleges and universities offer classes in computer basics, as well as more advanced topics like programming and web design.
- Practice: The best way to learn is by doing. Try to find opportunities to practice your computer skills, such as creating a document or designing a website.

- Read: Reading books and articles about computer skills can help you learn more about the topic.
- Ask questions: Don't be afraid to ask questions if you don't understand something. There are many online forums and communities where you can get help from experienced computer users.

WHAT ARE THE BENEFITS OF HAVING GOOD COMPUTER SKILLS?

Having good computer skills can open up a world of opportunities. Here are some of the benefits of having good computer skills:

- Increased productivity: Having good computer skills can help you work more efficiently and get more done in less time.
- Improved communication: Good computer skills can help you communicate more effectively with colleagues, customers, and other stakeholders.
- Increased job opportunities: Having good computer skills can make you more attractive to potential employers.
- Improved problem-solving skills: Good computer skills can help you think more critically and solve problems more effectively.

CONCLUSION

Having basic computer skills is essential for success in today's digital world. From basic word processing to more advanced tasks like coding and web design, having a good grasp of computer skills can open up a world of opportunities. Developing your computer skills is an ongoing process, but with the right resources and practice, you can become a computer whiz in no time.

Q: What are basic computer skills?

A: Basic computer skills are the fundamental abilities and knowledge needed to use a computer. These skills include the ability to navigate a computer's operating system, use basic programs, and troubleshoot common problems.

Q: What are the different types of computer skills?

A: There are many different types of computer skills, including operating system skills, word processing skills, spreadsheet skills, database skills, programming skills, web design skills, networking skills, and troubleshooting skills.

Q: How can I develop my computer skills?

A: Developing your computer skills is an ongoing process. You can take a class, practice, read, and ask questions to help you learn more about computer skills.

Q: What are the benefits of having good computer skills?

A: Having good computer skills can increase your productivity, improve your communication, open up job opportunities, and help you think more critically and solve problems more effectively.

Q: What resources can I use to learn more about computer skills?

A: There are many resources available to help you learn more about computer skills, including online classes, books, articles, and online forums and communities.

HOW TO HANDLE STRESS

STRESS MANAGEMENT STRATEGIES FOR A HEALTHIER LIFE

Stress is a normal part of life, but it can become overwhelming and have a negative impact on our physical and mental health. Fortunately, there are many strategies that can help us manage stress and lead a healthier life. In this article, we will discuss some of the most effective stress management strategies and how to implement them in our daily lives.

IDENTIFYING THE SOURCES OF STRESS

The first step in managing stress is to identify the sources of stress in our lives. This can be done by keeping a journal and writing down the events and situations that cause us stress. Once we have identified the sources of stress, we can begin to develop strategies to manage them.

DEVELOPING HEALTHY COPING STRATEGIES

Once we have identified the sources of stress, we can begin to develop healthy coping strategies. These strategies can include relaxation techniques such as deep breathing, progressive muscle relaxation, and mindfulness meditation. We can also practice positive self-talk and reframe negative thoughts. Additionally, we can engage in physical activities such as walking, running, or yoga to help reduce stress.

MAKING TIME FOR SELF-CARE

In addition to developing healthy coping strategies, it is important to make time for self-care. This can include activities such as getting enough sleep, eating a healthy diet, and engaging in activities that bring us joy. Taking time for ourselves can help us to reduce stress and feel more balanced.

SEEKING PROFESSIONAL HELP

If we are struggling to manage our stress, it is important to seek professional help. A mental health professional can help us to identify the sources of our stress and develop strategies to manage it. They can also provide support and guidance as we work to reduce our stress levels.

PRACTICING STRESS MANAGEMENT TECHNIQUES

Once we have identified the sources of stress and developed strategies to manage it, it is important to practice these techniques on a regular basis. This can include relaxation techniques, positive self-talk, and engaging in physical activities. Practicing these techniques can help us to reduce our stress levels and lead a healthier life.

CONCLUSION

Stress is a normal part of life, but it can become overwhelming and have a negative impact on our physical and mental health. Fortunately, there are many strategies that can help us manage stress and lead a healthier life. By identifying the sources of stress, developing healthy coping strategies, making time for self-care, and seeking professional help, we can reduce our stress levels and lead a healthier life.

Q: What are some effective stress management strategies?

A: Some effective stress management strategies include relaxation techniques such as deep breathing, progressive muscle relaxation, and mindfulness meditation. Additionally, engaging in physical activities such as walking, running, or yoga can help reduce stress. Making time for self-care and seeking professional help can also be beneficial.

Q: How can I identify the sources of stress in my life?

A: One way to identify the sources of stress in your life is to keep a journal and write down the events and situations that cause you stress. Once you have identified the sources of stress, you can begin to develop strategies to manage them.

Q: How often should I practice stress management techniques?

A: It is important to practice stress management techniques on a regular basis in order to reduce stress levels and lead a healthier life. This can include relaxation techniques, positive self-talk, and engaging in physical activities.

Q: What should I do if I am struggling to manage my stress?

A: If you are struggling to manage your stress, it is important to seek professional help. A mental health professional can help you to identify the sources of your stress and develop strategies to manage it.

Q: What are some activities that can help reduce stress?

A: Some activities that can help reduce stress include relaxation techniques such as deep breathing, progressive muscle relaxation, and mindfulness meditation. Additionally, engaging in physical activities such as walking, running, or yoga can help reduce stress. Making time for self-care and seeking professional help can also be beneficial.

BASIC LEGAL KNOWLEDGE: WHAT YOU NEED TO KNOW

Legal knowledge is essential for anyone who wants to stay on the right side of the law. Whether you're a business owner, an employee, or a student, understanding the basics of the law can help you make informed decisions and protect your rights. In this article, we'll discuss the basics of legal knowledge and why it's important.

WHAT IS LEGAL KNOWLEDGE?

Legal knowledge is the understanding of the laws and regulations that govern a particular jurisdiction. It includes an understanding of the legal system, the rights and responsibilities of citizens, and the legal processes that are used to resolve disputes. Legal knowledge is essential for anyone who wants to stay on the right side of the law.

WHY IS LEGAL KNOWLEDGE IMPORTANT?

Legal knowledge is important for a variety of reasons. First, it helps individuals and businesses understand their rights and responsibilities under the law. This can help them make informed decisions and protect their rights. Second, legal knowledge can help individuals and businesses avoid costly legal disputes. Third, legal knowledge can help individuals and businesses understand the legal process and how to navigate it. Finally, legal knowledge can help individuals and businesses understand the consequences of their actions and how to avoid them.

WHAT ARE THE BASICS OF LEGAL KNOWLEDGE?

The basics of legal knowledge include an understanding of the legal system, the rights and responsibilities of citizens, and the legal processes that are used to resolve disputes. It also includes an understanding of the different types of laws, such as criminal, civil, and administrative law. Additionally, it includes an understanding of the different types of legal documents, such as contracts, wills, and trusts.

HOW CAN I LEARN MORE ABOUT LEGAL KNOWLEDGE?

There are a variety of ways to learn more about legal knowledge. You can take classes at a local college or university, attend seminars or workshops, or read books and articles about the law. Additionally, you can consult with a lawyer or other legal professional to get advice and guidance.

WHAT ARE THE BENEFITS OF HAVING LEGAL KNOWLEDGE?

Having legal knowledge can provide a variety of benefits. It can help individuals and businesses understand their rights and responsibilities under the law. It can also help them make informed decisions and protect their rights. Additionally, it can help them avoid costly legal disputes and understand the legal process and how to navigate it.

Finally, it can help them understand the consequences of their actions and how to avoid them.

CONCLUSION

Legal knowledge is essential for anyone who wants to stay on the right side of the law. It includes an understanding of the legal system, the rights and responsibilities of citizens, and the legal processes that are used to resolve disputes. There are a variety of ways to learn more about legal knowledge, such as taking classes, attending seminars or workshops, or consulting with a lawyer or other legal professional. Having legal knowledge can provide a variety of benefits, such as helping individuals and businesses understand their rights and responsibilities under the law, make informed decisions, and protect their rights.

Q: What is legal knowledge?

A: Legal knowledge is the understanding of the laws and regulations that govern a particular jurisdiction. It includes an understanding of the legal system, the rights and responsibilities of citizens, and the legal processes that are used to resolve disputes.

Q: Why is legal knowledge important?

A: Legal knowledge is important for a variety of reasons. It helps individuals and businesses understand their rights and responsibilities under the law, make informed decisions, and protect their rights. It can also help them avoid costly legal disputes and understand the legal process and how to navigate it.

Q: What are the basics of legal knowledge?

A: The basics of legal knowledge include an understanding of the legal system, the rights and responsibilities of citizens, and the legal processes that are used to resolve disputes. It also includes an understanding of the different types of laws, such as criminal, civil, and administrative law. Additionally, it includes an understanding of the different types of legal documents, such as contracts, wills, and trusts.

Q: How can I learn more about legal knowledge?

A: There are a variety of ways to learn more about legal knowledge. You can take classes at a local college or university, attend seminars or workshops, or read books and articles about the law. Additionally, you can consult with a lawyer or other legal professional to get advice and guidance.

Q: What are the benefits of having legal knowledge?

A: Having legal knowledge can provide a variety of benefits. It can help individuals and businesses understand their rights and responsibilities under the law. It can also help them make informed decisions and protect their rights. Additionally, it can help them avoid costly legal disputes and understand the legal process and how to navigate it. Finally, it can help them understand the consequences of their actions and how to avoid them.

KNOWLEDGE OF PERSONAL HEALTH: A COMPREHENSIVE GUIDE

INTRODUCTION TO PERSONAL HEALTH

Personal health is an important part of our lives. It is the foundation of our physical, mental, and emotional wellbeing. It is essential to understand the basics of personal health in order to maintain a healthy lifestyle. This comprehensive guide will provide an overview of personal health, including its definition, components, and benefits.

WHAT IS PERSONAL HEALTH?

Personal health is the state of physical, mental, and emotional wellbeing. It is the result of a combination of factors, including lifestyle choices, genetics, and environmental influences. Personal health is not just about physical health, but also includes mental and emotional health.

COMPONENTS OF PERSONAL HEALTH

Personal health is composed of several components, including physical health, mental health, and emotional health. Physical health is the state of the body, including its physical condition, strength, and endurance. Mental health is the state of the mind, including its ability to think, reason, and remember. Emotional health is the state of the emotions, including the ability to cope with stress and express feelings.

BENEFITS OF PERSONAL HEALTH

Personal health has many benefits, including improved physical and mental wellbeing, increased energy levels, and improved quality of life. Good physical health can help reduce the risk of chronic diseases, such as heart disease and diabetes. Good mental health can help reduce stress and anxiety and improve cognitive functioning. Good emotional health can help improve relationships and communication skills.

TIPS FOR IMPROVING PERSONAL HEALTH

There are several steps that can be taken to improve personal health. Eating a balanced diet, exercising regularly, and getting enough sleep are all important for maintaining physical health. Practicing relaxation techniques, such as yoga and meditation, can help improve mental and emotional health. Additionally, it is important to stay connected with friends and family, and to seek help from a mental health professional if needed.

CONCLUSION

Personal health is an important part of our lives. It is essential to understand the basics of personal health in order to maintain a healthy lifestyle. Good personal health can have many benefits, including improved physical and mental wellbeing, increased energy levels, and improved quality of life. There are several steps that can be taken to improve personal health, such as eating a balanced diet, exercising regularly, and getting enough sleep. Additionally, it is important to stay connected with friends and family, and to seek help from a mental health professional if needed.

Q: What is personal health?

A: Personal health is the state of physical, mental, and emotional wellbeing. It is the result of a combination of factors, including lifestyle choices, genetics, and environmental influences.

Q: What are the components of personal health?

A: The components of personal health include physical health, mental health, and emotional health.

Q: What are the benefits of personal health?

A: The benefits of personal health include improved physical and mental wellbeing, increased energy levels, and improved quality of life.

Q: What are some tips for improving personal health?

A: Some tips for improving personal health include eating a balanced diet, exercising regularly, getting enough sleep, practicing relaxation techniques, and staying connected with friends and family.

Q: When should I seek help from a mental health professional?

A: If you are struggling with mental health issues, it is important to seek help from a mental health professional.

SELF-AWARENESS: A COMPREHENSIVE GUIDE

WHAT IS SELF AWARENESS?

Self awareness is the ability to recognize and understand one's own emotions, thoughts, and behaviors. It is the capacity to be conscious of one's own character, feelings, and motivations. Self awareness is the foundation of emotional intelligence, and it is essential for personal growth and development.

BENEFITS OF SELF AWARENESS

Self awareness is a key component of emotional intelligence, and it can have a profound impact on our lives. It can help us to better understand our own emotions, thoughts, and behaviors, and it can also help us to better understand the emotions, thoughts, and behaviors of others. Self awareness can help us to make better decisions, to be more successful in our relationships, and to be more effective in our work.

HOW TO DEVELOP SELF AWARENESS

Developing self awareness is a process that requires time and effort. It involves learning to recognize and understand our own emotions, thoughts, and behaviors, and it also involves learning to recognize and understand the emotions, thoughts, and behaviors of others. Here are some tips for developing self awareness:

- Take time to reflect on your thoughts and feelings.
- Pay attention to your body language and facial expressions.
- Listen to your inner voice and be mindful of your reactions.
- Practice self-compassion and self-care.
- Seek feedback from others.
- Spend time in nature and practice mindfulness.
- Read books and articles about self awareness.
- Practice meditation and yoga.
- Journal your thoughts and feelings.

CHALLENGES OF SELF AWARENESS

Developing self awareness can be a challenging process. It can be difficult to recognize and understand our own emotions, thoughts, and behaviors, and it can also be difficult to recognize and understand the emotions, thoughts, and behaviors of others. It can also be difficult to accept our own flaws and weaknesses, and it can be difficult to accept the flaws and weaknesses of others.

SELF AWARENESS AND RELATIONSHIPS

Self awareness is essential for healthy relationships. It can help us to better understand our own emotions, thoughts, and behaviors, and it can also help us to better understand the emotions, thoughts, and behaviors of others. Self awareness can help us to communicate more effectively, to resolve conflicts more peacefully, and to build stronger, more meaningful relationships.

SELF AWARENESS AND MENTAL HEALTH

Self awareness is also essential for mental health. It can help us to recognize and understand our own emotions, thoughts, and behaviors, and it can also help us to recognize and understand the emotions, thoughts, and behaviors of others. Self awareness can help us to identify and address mental health issues, to cope with stress and anxiety, and to build resilience.

SELF AWARENESS AND PERSONAL GROWTH

Self awareness is essential for personal growth and development. It can help us to recognize and understand our own emotions, thoughts, and behaviors, and it can also help us to recognize and understand the emotions, thoughts, and behaviors of others. Self awareness can help us to identify our strengths and weaknesses, to set goals and achieve them, and to become the best version of ourselves.

SELF AWARENESS AND SUCCESS

Self awareness is essential for success. It can help us to recognize and understand our own emotions, thoughts, and behaviors, and it can also help us to recognize and understand the emotions, thoughts, and behaviors of others. Self awareness can help us to make better decisions, to be more effective in our work, and to achieve our goals.

CONCLUSION

Self awareness is an essential skill for personal growth and development, for healthy relationships, for mental health, and for success. It involves learning to recognize and understand our own emotions, thoughts, and behaviors, and it also involves learning to recognize and understand the emotions, thoughts, and behaviors of others. Developing self awareness is a process that requires time and effort, but it can have a profound impact on our lives.

Q: What is self awareness?

A: Self awareness is the ability to recognize and understand one's own emotions, thoughts, and behaviors. It is the capacity to be conscious of one's own character, feelings, and motivations.

Q: What are the benefits of self awareness?

A: Self awareness can help us to make better decisions, to be more successful in our relationships, and to be more effective in our work.

Q: How can I develop self awareness?

A: Developing self awareness involves taking time to reflect on your thoughts and feelings, paying attention to your body language and facial expressions, listening to your inner voice, practicing self-compassion and self-care, seeking feedback from others, spending time in nature and practicing mindfulness, reading books and articles about self awareness, practicing meditation and yoga, and journaling your thoughts and feelings.

Q: What are the challenges of self awareness?

A: Developing self awareness can be a challenging process. It can be difficult to recognize and understand our own emotions, thoughts, and behaviors, and it can also be difficult to recognize and understand the emotions, thoughts, and behaviors of others. It can also be difficult to accept our own flaws and weaknesses, and it can be difficult to accept the flaws and weaknesses of others.

Q: How can self awareness help me in my relationships and in my work?

A: Self awareness can help us to better understand our own emotions, thoughts, and behaviors, and it can also help us to better understand the emotions, thoughts, and behaviors of others. Self awareness can help us to communicate more effectively, to resolve conflicts more peacefully, and to build stronger, more meaningful relationships. It can also help us to make better decisions, to be more effective in our work, and to achieve our goals.

THE POWER OF COMPOUND INTEREST

Compound interest is one of the most powerful financial tools available to individuals and businesses. It is a form of interest that is calculated on the initial principal and also on the accumulated interest of previous periods. Compound interest can be used to generate wealth over time, and it is a key component of many investment strategies.

WHAT IS COMPOUND INTEREST?

Compound interest is a type of interest that is calculated on the initial principal and also on the accumulated interest of previous periods. It is a powerful financial tool that can be used to generate wealth over time. Compound interest is calculated by multiplying the principal amount by one plus the annual interest rate raised to the number of compound periods minus one.

For example, if you invest $1,000 at an annual interest rate of 5%, compounded monthly, the calculation would be:

$1,000 x (1 + 0.05/12)^{12} - 1 = $1,051.45

This means that after one year, your investment would be worth $1,051.45.

HOW DOES COMPOUND INTEREST WORK?

Compound interest works by reinvesting the interest earned on an investment. This means that the interest earned on the initial investment is added to the principal amount, and then the interest is calculated on the new, larger principal amount. This process is repeated over time, resulting in exponential growth of the investment.

The power of compound interest lies in its ability to generate wealth over time. The longer the investment is held, the more powerful the effect of compound interest becomes. For example, if you invest $1,000 at an annual interest rate of 5%, compounded monthly, after 10 years your investment would be worth $1,628.89. After 20 years, it would be worth $2,653.33.

THE BENEFITS OF COMPOUND INTEREST

Compound interest can be a powerful tool for generating wealth over time. It is a key component of many investment strategies, and it can be used to achieve financial goals such as retirement savings or college tuition.

Compound interest can also be used to reduce debt. By making regular payments on a loan or credit card balance, the interest earned on the payments is added to the principal amount, resulting in a faster repayment of the debt.

THE DRAWBACKS OF COMPOUND INTEREST

Compound interest can be a powerful tool for generating wealth, but it can also be a double-edged sword. If you are investing in a high-risk investment, the potential for losses can be magnified by the power of compound interest.

In addition, compound interest can be difficult to understand and calculate. It is important to understand the terms of any investment before investing, and to be aware of the potential risks.

CONCLUSION

Compound interest is a powerful financial tool that can be used to generate wealth over time. It is a key component of many investment strategies, and it can be used to achieve financial goals such as retirement savings or college tuition. However, it is important to understand the terms of any investment before investing, and to be aware of the potential risks. With a thorough understanding of compound interest and a sound investment strategy, it is possible to take advantage of the power of compound interest to achieve financial success.

Q: What is compound interest?

A: Compound interest is a type of interest that is calculated on the initial principal and also on the accumulated interest of previous periods. It is a powerful financial tool that can be used to generate wealth over time.

Q: How does compound interest work?

A: Compound interest works by reinvesting the interest earned on an investment. This means that the interest earned on the initial investment is added to the principal amount, and then the interest is calculated on the new, larger principal amount. This process is repeated over time, resulting in exponential growth of the investment.

Q: What are the benefits of compound interest?

A: Compound interest can be a powerful tool for generating wealth over time. It is a key component of many investment strategies, and it can be used to achieve financial goals such as retirement savings or college tuition. Compound interest can also be used to reduce debt.

Q: What are the drawbacks of compound interest?

A: Compound interest can be a powerful tool for generating wealth, but it can also be a double-edged sword. If you are investing in a high-risk investment, the potential for losses can be magnified by the power of compound interest. In addition, compound interest can be difficult to understand and calculate.

Q: How is compound interest calculated?

A: Compound interest is calculated by multiplying the principal amount by one plus the annual interest rate raised to the number of compound periods minus one. For example, if you invest $1,000 at an annual interest rate of 5%, compounded monthly, the calculation would be: $1,000 \times (1 + 0.05/12)^{12} - 1 = \$1,051.45$. This means that after one year, your investment would be worth $1,051.45.

HOW TO STOP LIVING PAYCHECK TO PAYCHECK

Living paycheck to paycheck is a common problem for many people. It can be a difficult cycle to break, but it is possible. With the right strategies and a bit of discipline, you can break the cycle and start building financial security. In this article, we'll discuss how to stop living paycheck to paycheck and start building a secure financial future.

WHAT DOES IT MEAN TO LIVE PAYCHECK TO PAYCHECK?

Living paycheck to paycheck means that you are relying on your current income to cover your expenses. You may not have any savings or investments, and you may be struggling to make ends meet. This can be a difficult situation to be in, as it can be hard to break the cycle and start building financial security.

WHY DO PEOPLE LIVE PAYCHECK TO PAYCHECK?

There are many reasons why people may find themselves living paycheck to paycheck. Some of the most common reasons include:

- Low wages: Low wages can make it difficult to save money and build financial security.

- High expenses: High expenses, such as rent, utilities, and other bills, can make it difficult to save money.
- Poor budgeting: Poor budgeting can lead to overspending and not having enough money to cover expenses.
- Unforeseen expenses: Unexpected expenses, such as medical bills or car repairs, can make it difficult to save money.

HOW TO STOP LIVING PAYCHECK TO PAYCHECK

Breaking the cycle of living paycheck to paycheck can be difficult, but it is possible. Here are some tips to help you get started:

- Create a budget: Creating a budget is the first step to breaking the cycle of living paycheck to paycheck. A budget will help you track your income and expenses, and it will help you identify areas where you can cut back.
- Cut back on expenses: Once you have created a budget, you can start to identify areas where you can cut back on expenses. This could include cutting back on eating out, reducing your entertainment expenses, or canceling unnecessary subscriptions.
- Increase your income: Increasing your income can help you break the cycle of living paycheck to paycheck. You could look for a higher-paying job, start a side hustle, or look for ways to increase your income from your current job.
- Start an emergency fund: An emergency fund is a savings account that you can use to cover unexpected expenses. Having an emergency fund can help you

avoid going into debt when unexpected expenses arise.

- Invest: Investing is a great way to build wealth and financial security. Investing can help you grow your money over time, and it can help you reach your financial goals.

CONCLUSION

Living paycheck to paycheck can be a difficult cycle to break, but it is possible. With the right strategies and a bit of discipline, you can break the cycle and start building financial security. Creating a budget, cutting back on expenses, increasing your income, starting an emergency fund, and investing are all great ways to start building financial security.

Q: How can I break the cycle of living paycheck to paycheck?

A: Breaking the cycle of living paycheck to paycheck can be difficult, but it is possible. Creating a budget, cutting back on expenses, increasing your income, starting an emergency fund, and investing are all great ways to start building financial security.

Q: What are some ways to increase my income?

A: There are many ways to increase your income. You could look for a higher-paying job, start a side hustle, or look for ways to increase your income from your current job.

Q: What is an emergency fund?

A: An emergency fund is a savings account that you can use to cover unexpected expenses. Having an emergency fund can help you avoid going into debt when unexpected expenses arise.

Q: How can I start investing?

A: Investing can be a great way to build wealth and financial security. You can start investing by opening an investment account with a broker or robo-advisor. You can also invest in stocks, bonds, mutual funds, and other investments.

Q: What are some tips for creating a budget?

A: Creating a budget is an important step to breaking the cycle of living paycheck to paycheck. Some tips for creating a budget include tracking your income and expenses, setting realistic goals, and creating a plan to reach those goals. You should also review your budget regularly to make sure you are staying on track.

THE IMPORTANCE OF DELAYED GRATIFICATION

Delayed gratification is a concept that has been around for centuries, but it has become increasingly important in today's world. It is the idea that you should wait to receive a reward or benefit until after you have put in the effort to achieve it. This concept is especially important in the modern world, where instant gratification is often the norm.

WHAT IS DELAYED GRATIFICATION?

Delayed gratification is the practice of waiting to receive a reward or benefit until after you have put in the effort to achieve it. It is the opposite of instant gratification, which is the idea that you should receive a reward or benefit immediately after you have put in the effort to achieve it.

Delayed gratification is a concept that has been around for centuries, but it has become increasingly important in today's world. It is the idea that you should wait to receive a reward or benefit until after you have put in the effort to achieve it. This concept is especially important in the modern world, where instant gratification is often the norm.

BENEFITS OF DELAYED GRATIFICATION

Delayed gratification has many benefits, both in the short-term and the long-term. In the short-term, it can help you stay focused on your goals and avoid distractions. It can also help you develop self-discipline and self-control, which are important skills for success.

In the long-term, delayed gratification can help you achieve your goals more quickly and efficiently. It can also help you develop a sense of satisfaction and accomplishment, as you will have worked hard to achieve your goals.

HOW TO PRACTICE DELAYED GRATIFICATION

Practicing delayed gratification can be difficult, especially in a world where instant gratification is often the norm. However, there are several strategies that can help you practice delayed gratification.

First, it is important to set realistic goals and timelines for yourself. This will help you stay focused and motivated to achieve your goals.

Second, it is important to practice self-discipline and self-control. This means avoiding distractions and temptations that could derail your progress.

Third, it is important to reward yourself for your efforts. This will help you stay motivated and remind you of the benefits of delayed gratification.

EXAMPLES OF DELAYED GRATIFICATION

There are many examples of delayed gratification in everyday life. For example, saving money for a vacation or a new car is an example of delayed gratification. Investing in stocks or mutual funds is another example of delayed gratification.

Delayed gratification can also be seen in the workplace. For example, working hard to get a promotion or a raise is an example of delayed gratification. Working hard to complete a project or to learn a new skill is another example of delayed gratification.

THE IMPORTANCE OF DELAYED GRATIFICATION

Delayed gratification is an important concept in today's world. It can help you stay focused on your goals and avoid distractions. It can also help you develop self-discipline and self-control, which are important skills for success.

In the long-term, delayed gratification can help you achieve your goals more quickly and efficiently. It can also help you develop a sense of satisfaction and accomplishment, as you will have worked hard to achieve your goals.

CONCLUSION

Delayed gratification is an important concept in today's world. It can help you stay focused on your goals and avoid distractions. It can also help you develop self-discipline and self-control, which are important skills for success. By practicing delayed gratification, you can achieve your goals more quickly and efficiently, and you can also develop a sense of satisfaction and accomplishment.

Q: What is delayed gratification?

A: Delayed gratification is the practice of waiting to receive a reward or benefit until after you have put in the effort to achieve it. It is the opposite of instant gratification, which is the idea that you should receive a reward or benefit immediately after you have put in the effort to achieve it.

Q: What are the benefits of delayed gratification?

A: Delayed gratification has many benefits, both in the short-term and the long-term. In the short-term, it can help you stay focused on your goals and avoid distractions. It can also help you develop self-discipline and self-control, which are important skills for success. In the long-term, delayed gratification can help you achieve your goals more quickly and efficiently. It can also help you develop a sense of satisfaction and accomplishment, as you will have worked hard to achieve your goals.

Q: How can I practice delayed gratification?

A: Practicing delayed gratification can be difficult, especially in a world where instant gratification is often the norm. However, there are several strategies that can help you practice delayed gratification. First, it is important to set realistic goals and timelines for yourself. This will help you stay focused and motivated to achieve your goals.

Second, it is important to practice self-discipline and self-control. This means avoiding distractions and temptations that could derail your progress. Third, it is important to reward yourself for your efforts. This will help you stay motivated and remind you of the benefits of delayed gratification.

Q: What are some examples of delayed gratification?

A: There are many examples of delayed gratification in everyday life. For example, saving money for a vacation or a new car is an example of delayed gratification. Investing in stocks or mutual funds is another example of delayed gratification. Delayed gratification can also be seen in the workplace. For example, working hard to get a promotion or a raise is an example of delayed gratification. Working hard to complete a project or to learn a new skill is another example of delayed gratification.

Q: Why is delayed gratification important?

A: Delayed gratification is an important concept in today's world. It can help you stay focused on your goals and avoid distractions. It can also help you develop self-discipline and self-control, which are important skills for success. In the long-term, delayed gratification can help you achieve your goals more quickly and efficiently. It can also help you develop a sense of satisfaction and accomplishment, as you will have worked hard to achieve your goals.

THE RULE OF 72: HOW TO DOUBLE YOUR MONEY IN JUST 7 YEARS

The Rule of 72 is a simple mathematical formula that can help you calculate how long it will take to double your money. It is a useful tool for investors, as it can help them determine how long it will take to reach their financial goals. The Rule of 72 is based on the concept of compound interest, which is the interest earned on the principal plus any interest earned on the interest.

The Rule of 72 states that if you divide 72 by the annual rate of return, you will get the number of years it will take to double your money. For example, if you invest $1,000 at an annual rate of return of 8%, it will take 9 years to double your money (72/8 = 9).

WHAT IS THE RULE OF 72?

The Rule of 72 is a simple mathematical formula that can help you calculate how long it will take to double your money. It is based on the concept of compound interest, which is the interest earned on the principal plus any interest earned on the interest. The Rule of 72 states that if you divide 72 by the annual rate of return, you will get the number of years it will take to double your money.

HOW DOES THE RULE OF 72 WORK?

The Rule of 72 works by taking the annual rate of return and dividing it into 72. For example, if you invest $1,000 at an annual rate of return of 8%, it will take 9 years to double your money (72/8 = 9). The higher the rate of return, the faster your money will double.

WHAT ARE THE BENEFITS OF USING THE RULE OF 72?

The Rule of 72 is a useful tool for investors, as it can help them determine how long it will take to reach their financial goals. It can also help investors decide which investments are best for their needs. For example, if an investor is looking for a long-term investment, they may want to choose an investment with a higher rate of return, as it will take less time to double their money.

WHAT ARE THE RISKS OF USING THE RULE OF 72?

The Rule of 72 is a useful tool, but it is important to remember that it is based on the concept of compound interest, which means that the rate of return is not guaranteed. The rate of return can fluctuate, which means that the amount of time it takes to double your money can also fluctuate. It is important to remember that investing involves risk, and that the rate of return is not guaranteed.

HOW CAN I USE THE RULE OF 72 TO REACH MY FINANCIAL GOALS?

The Rule of 72 can be used to help you reach your financial goals. By calculating the number of years, it will take to double your money, you can determine how long it will take to reach your financial goals. You can also use the

Rule of 72 to compare different investments and decide which one is best for your needs.

CONCLUSION

The Rule of 72 is a simple mathematical formula that can help you calculate how long it will take to double your money. It is based on the concept of compound interest, which is the interest earned on the principal plus any interest earned on the interest. The Rule of 72 is a useful tool for investors, as it can help them determine how long it will take to reach their financial goals. It can also help investors decide which investments are best for their needs. However, it is important to remember that investing involves risk, and that the rate of return is not guaranteed.

Q: What is the Rule of 72?

A: The Rule of 72 is a simple mathematical formula that can help you calculate how long it will take to double your money. It is based on the concept of compound interest, which is the interest earned on the principal plus any interest earned on the interest.

Q: How Does the Rule of 72 Work?

A: The Rule of 72 works by taking the annual rate of return and dividing it into 72. For example, if you invest $1,000 at an annual rate of return of 8%, it will take 9 years to double your money (72/8 = 9).

Q: What Are the Benefits of Using the Rule of 72?

A: The Rule of 72 is a useful tool for investors, as it can help them determine how long it will take to reach their financial goals. It can also help investors decide which investments are best for their needs.

Q: What Are the Risks of Using the Rule of 72?

A: The Rule of 72 is a useful tool, but it is important to remember that it is based on the concept of compound interest, which means that the rate of return is not guaranteed. The rate of return can fluctuate, which means that the amount of time it takes to double your money can also fluctuate.

Q: How Can I Use the Rule of 72 to Reach My Financial Goals?

A: The Rule of 72 can be used to help you reach your financial goals. By calculating the number of years, it will take to double your money, you can determine how long it will take to reach your financial goals. You can also use the Rule of 72 to compare different investments and decide which one is best for your needs.

EXECUTING ESSENTIAL LEGAL DOCUMENTS

Legal documents are an important part of any business or personal transaction. They provide a written record of the agreement between two or more parties, and they can be used to protect the rights of all involved. Executing essential legal documents is a critical step in any transaction, and it is important to understand the process and the implications of signing a document.

WHAT IS AN ESSENTIAL LEGAL DOCUMENT?

An essential legal document is a document that is legally binding and enforceable. It is a written agreement between two or more parties that outlines the terms and conditions of a transaction. Essential legal documents can include contracts, wills, trusts, deeds, and other documents that are used to protect the rights of all involved.

WHAT IS THE PROCESS FOR EXECUTING ESSENTIAL LEGAL DOCUMENTS?

The process for executing essential legal documents varies depending on the type of document and the parties involved. Generally, the process involves the following steps:

1. Negotiate the terms of the document.

2. Draft the document.
3. Review the document.
4. Sign the document.
5. Notarize the document.
6. File the document.

WHAT ARE THE IMPLICATIONS OF EXECUTING ESSENTIAL LEGAL DOCUMENTS?

Executing essential legal documents can have serious implications for all parties involved. It is important to understand the terms of the document and the potential consequences of signing it. Once a document is signed, it is legally binding and enforceable. This means that all parties must abide by the terms of the document or face legal consequences.

WHAT ARE THE BENEFITS OF EXECUTING ESSENTIAL LEGAL DOCUMENTS?

Executing essential legal documents can provide a number of benefits for all parties involved. It can provide a written record of the agreement between two or more parties, which can be used to protect the rights of all involved. It can also provide clarity and certainty in a transaction, which can help to avoid disputes and misunderstandings.

WHAT ARE THE RISKS OF EXECUTING ESSENTIAL LEGAL DOCUMENTS?

Executing essential legal documents can also carry certain risks. It is important to understand the terms of the document and the potential consequences of signing it. If the document is not properly drafted or reviewed, it can lead to disputes and misunderstandings. It is also important to ensure that all parties understand the terms of the document and are willing to abide by them.

WHAT ARE THE BEST PRACTICES FOR EXECUTING ESSENTIAL LEGAL DOCUMENTS?

The best practices for executing essential legal documents include:

1. Negotiate the terms of the document.
2. Draft the document.
3. Review the document.
4. Sign the document.
5. Notarize the document.
6. File the document.
7. Ensure that all parties understand the terms of the document.
8. Ensure that all parties are willing to abide by the terms of the document.
9. Ensure that the document is properly drafted and reviewed.
10. Ensure that the document is legally binding and enforceable.

CONCLUSION:

Executing essential legal documents is a critical step in any transaction. It is important to understand the process and the implications of signing a document. It is also important to ensure that all parties understand the terms of the document and are willing to abide by them. By following the best practices for executing essential legal documents, all parties can ensure that their rights are protected, and that the transaction is legally binding and enforceable.

Q: What is an essential legal document?

A: An essential legal document is a document that is legally binding and enforceable. It is a written agreement between two or more parties that outlines the terms and conditions of a transaction. Essential legal documents can include contracts, wills, trusts, deeds, and other documents.

Q: What is the process for executing essential legal documents?

A: The process for executing essential legal documents varies depending on the type of document and the parties involved. Generally, the process involves negotiating the terms of the document, drafting the document, reviewing the document, signing the document, notarizing the document, and filing the document.

Q: What are the implications of executing essential legal documents?

A: Executing essential legal documents can have serious implications for all parties involved. It is important to understand the terms of the document and the potential consequences of signing it. Once a document is signed, it is legally binding and enforceable. This means that all parties must abide by the terms of the document or face legal consequences.

Q: What are the benefits of executing essential legal documents?

A: Executing essential legal documents can provide a number of benefits for all parties involved. It can provide a written record of the agreement between two or more parties, which can be used to protect the rights of all involved. It can also provide clarity and certainty in a transaction, which can help to avoid disputes and misunderstandings.

Q: What are the best practices for executing essential legal documents?

A: The best practices for executing essential legal documents include negotiating the terms of the document, drafting the document, reviewing the document, signing the document, notarizing the document, filing the document, ensuring that all parties understand the terms of the document, ensuring that all parties are willing to abide by the terms of the document, ensuring that the document is properly drafted and reviewed, and ensuring that the document is legally binding and enforceable.

HOW TO KEEP YOUR COMPUTER SECURE

In today's digital world, it is essential to keep your computer secure. With the rise of cybercrime, it is more important than ever to ensure that your computer is protected from malicious attacks. In this article, we will discuss the steps you can take to keep your computer secure and protect your data.

WHAT IS COMPUTER SECURITY?

Computer security is the practice of protecting your computer from malicious attacks. It involves the use of software, hardware, and other measures to protect your computer from viruses, malware, and other threats. It also involves the use of encryption and other measures to protect your data from unauthorized access.

WHY IS COMPUTER SECURITY IMPORTANT?

Computer security is important because it helps protect your data from unauthorized access. It also helps protect your computer from malicious attacks, such as viruses, malware, and other threats. Without proper security measures, your computer and data could be vulnerable to attack.

WHAT ARE THE DIFFERENT TYPES OF COMPUTER SECURITY?

There are several different types of computer security. These include antivirus software, firewalls, encryption, and other measures. Antivirus software helps protect your computer from viruses and other malicious attacks. Firewalls help protect your computer from unauthorized access. Encryption helps protect your data from unauthorized access.

HOW CAN I KEEP MY COMPUTER SECURE?

There are several steps you can take to keep your computer secure. These include:

- Installing and regularly updating antivirus software
- Installing and regularly updating a firewall
- Using strong passwords
- Backing up your data regularly
- Using encryption
- Disabling unnecessary services
- Keeping your operating system and other software up to date

WHAT ARE THE BENEFITS OF KEEPING MY COMPUTER SECURE?

The benefits of keeping your computer secure include:

- Protecting your data from unauthorized access
- Protecting your computer from malicious attacks
- Keeping your computer running smoothly
- Preventing identity theft
- Protecting your online accounts

WHAT ARE THE RISKS OF NOT KEEPING MY COMPUTER SECURE?

The risks of not keeping your computer secure include:

- Loss of data
- Loss of privacy
- Loss of money
- Identity theft
- Malware infections
- Unauthorized access to your computer

CONCLUSION

Computer security is essential in today's digital world. It is important to take steps to protect your computer from malicious attacks and unauthorized access. Installing and regularly updating antivirus software, firewalls, and encryption are all important steps to take to keep your computer secure. Additionally, using strong passwords, backing up your data regularly, and keeping your operating system and other software up to date are all important steps to take to keep your computer secure.

Q: What is the best way to keep my computer secure?

A: The best way to keep your computer secure is to install and regularly update antivirus software, firewalls, and encryption. Additionally, using strong passwords, backing up your data regularly, and keeping your operating system and other software up to date are all important steps to take to keep your computer secure.

Q: What are the risks of not keeping my computer secure?

A: The risks of not keeping your computer secure include loss of data, loss of privacy, loss of money, identity theft, malware infections, and unauthorized access to your computer.

Q: What is the purpose of encryption?

A: The purpose of encryption is to protect your data from unauthorized access. Encryption scrambles your data so that it is unreadable to anyone who does not have the encryption key.

Q: What is the difference between antivirus software and a firewall?

A: Antivirus software helps protect your computer from viruses and other malicious attacks. A firewall helps protect your computer from unauthorized access.

Q: How often should I update my antivirus software?

A: You should update your antivirus software at least once a week. Additionally, you should update your antivirus software whenever a new version is released.

HOW TO MAKE MONEY WITHOUT A JOB

Making money without a job is a dream for many people. It can be a difficult task, but it is possible. With the right strategies and dedication, anyone can make money without a job. In this article, we will discuss the different ways to make money without a job, and how to make the most of them.

WHAT IS MAKING MONEY WITHOUT A JOB?

Making money without a job is the process of generating income without having to work a traditional job. This can be done through a variety of methods, such as freelancing, investing, or starting a business. It is important to note that making money without a job is not a get-rich-quick scheme, and it requires dedication and hard work.

BENEFITS OF MAKING MONEY WITHOUT A JOB

Making money without a job has many benefits. The most obvious benefit is that you don't have to work a traditional job. This means that you can have more freedom and flexibility in your life. You can also have more control over your income, as you can choose how much you want to make. Additionally, you can have more control over your time, as you can choose when and how you want to work.

DIFFERENT WAYS TO MAKE MONEY WITHOUT A JOB

There are many different ways to make money without a job. Some of the most popular methods include freelancing, investing, starting a business, and selling products online. Each of these methods has its own advantages and disadvantages, and it is important to research each one before deciding which one is right for you.

FREELANCING

Freelancing is one of the most popular ways to make money without a job. Freelancing involves providing services to clients on a contract basis. This can include writing, web design, graphic design, and many other services. Freelancing is a great way to make money without a job, as it allows you to work from home and set your own hours.

INVESTING

Investing is another popular way to make money without a job. Investing involves putting your money into stocks, bonds, mutual funds, and other investments. Investing can be a great way to make money without a job, as it allows you to make money without having to work. However, it is important to note that investing can be risky, and it is important to do your research before investing.

STARTING A BUSINESS

Starting a business is another way to make money without a job. Starting a business involves creating a product or service and selling it to customers. This can be a great way to make money without a job, as it allows you to be your own boss and have control over your income. However, starting a business can be risky, and it is important to do your research before starting one.

SELLING PRODUCTS ONLINE

Selling products online is another way to make money without a job. This involves creating or buying products and selling them online. This can be a great way to make money without a job, as it allows you to reach a global audience and make money without having to work. However, it is important to note that selling products online can be risky, and it is important to do your research before selling products online.

TIPS FOR MAKING MONEY WITHOUT A JOB

Making money without a job can be a difficult task, but it is possible. Here are some tips to help you make the most of your efforts:

- Research: It is important to do your research before deciding which method of making money without a job is right for you.
- Dedication: Making money without a job requires dedication and hard work. It is important to stay focused and motivated.
- Networking: Networking is an important part of making money without a job. It is important to build relationships with potential clients and customers.
- Patience: Making money without a job can take time. It is important to be patient and not give up.

CONCLUSION

Making money without a job is a difficult task, but it is possible. With the right strategies and dedication, anyone can make money without a job. There are many different ways to make money without a job, such as freelancing, investing, starting a business, and selling products online. It is important to do your research before deciding which method is right for you. With dedication and hard work, anyone can make money without a job.

Q: Is it possible to make money without a job?

Yes, it is possible to make money without a job. There are many different ways to make money without a job, such as freelancing, investing, starting a business, and selling products online.

Q: What are the benefits of making money without a job?

The benefits of making money without a job include more freedom and flexibility, more control over your income, and more control over your time.

Q: What are some tips for making money without a job?

Some tips for making money without a job include doing your research, staying dedicated and motivated, networking, and being patient.

Q: What are some of the most popular ways to make money without a job?

Some of the most popular ways to make money without a job include freelancing, investing, starting a business, and selling products online.

Q: How long does it take to make money without a job?

Making money without a job can take time, and it is important to be patient. It is important to stay dedicated and motivated, and to do your research before deciding which method is right for you.

SOFT SKILLS ARE ESSENTIAL

SOFT SKILLS ARE ESSENTIAL FOR PROFESSIONAL SUCCESS

Soft skills are essential for professional success in today's competitive job market. Soft skills are the personal attributes and qualities that enable an individual to interact effectively and harmoniously with other people. They are the skills that help you to communicate, collaborate, and work with others in a productive and efficient manner. Soft skills are the key to success in any job, and they are becoming increasingly important in the modern workplace.

Soft skills are the skills that employers look for when hiring new employees. They include communication, problem-solving, teamwork, leadership, and interpersonal skills. Soft skills are the skills that employers value most in their employees. They are the skills that make an employee stand out from the crowd and make them an asset to any organization.

WHAT ARE SOFT SKILLS?

Soft skills are the personal attributes and qualities that enable an individual to interact effectively and harmoniously with other people. They are the skills that help you to communicate, collaborate, and work with others in a productive and efficient manner. Soft skills are the key to success in any job, and they are becoming increasingly important in the modern workplace.

Soft skills are the skills that employers look for when hiring new employees. They include communication, problem-solving, teamwork, leadership, and interpersonal skills. Soft skills are the skills that employers value most in their employees. They are the skills that make an employee stand out from the crowd and make them an asset to any organization.

WHY ARE SOFT SKILLS IMPORTANT?

Soft skills are important because they help employees to work together effectively and efficiently. They are the skills that enable employees to communicate effectively, collaborate, and work together to achieve common goals. Soft skills are also important because they help employees to build relationships with their colleagues and customers.

Soft skills are important because they help employees to develop their professional skills and abilities. They are the skills that help employees to think critically, solve problems, and make decisions. Soft skills are also important because they help employees to develop their emotional intelligence and self-awareness.

HOW CAN YOU DEVELOP SOFT SKILLS?

Soft skills can be developed through practice and experience. It is important to practice communication, problem-solving, teamwork, leadership, and interpersonal skills in order to develop them. It is also important to take the time to reflect on your experiences and learn from them.

Soft skills can also be developed through formal education and training. There are many courses and programs available that can help you to develop your soft skills. It is also important to read books and articles about soft skills and to attend seminars and workshops on the topic.

WHAT ARE THE BENEFITS OF SOFT SKILLS?

Soft skills have many benefits for both employers and employees. They help employers to create a productive and efficient workplace. They also help employees to develop their professional skills and abilities.

Soft skills help employees to build relationships with their colleagues and customers. They also help employees to think critically, solve problems, and make decisions. Soft skills are also important because they help employees to develop their emotional intelligence and self-awareness.

HOW CAN SOFT SKILLS HELP YOU IN YOUR CAREER?

Soft skills can help you to stand out from the crowd and make you an asset to any organization. They are the skills that employers look for when hiring new employees. Soft skills can also help you to develop your professional skills and abilities.

Soft skills can also help you to build relationships with your colleagues and customers. They are the skills that enable you to communicate effectively, collaborate, and work together to achieve common goals. Soft skills are also important because they help you to develop your emotional intelligence and self-awareness.

WHAT ARE THE CHALLENGES OF DEVELOPING SOFT SKILLS?

Developing soft skills can be challenging because they require practice and experience. It is important to practice communication, problem-solving, teamwork, leadership, and interpersonal skills in order to develop them. It is also important to take the time to reflect on your experiences and learn from them.

Developing soft skills can also be challenging because they require formal education and training. There are many courses and programs available that can help you to develop your soft skills. It is also important to read books and articles about soft skills and to attend seminars and workshops on the topic.

CONCLUSION

Soft skills are essential for professional success in today's competitive job market. They are the skills that employers look for when hiring new employees. Soft skills are the key to success in any job, and they are becoming increasingly important in the modern workplace. Soft skills can be developed through practice and experience, as well as through formal education and training. They help employees to work together effectively and efficiently, and they help employees to build relationships with their colleagues and customers. Soft skills are the skills that make an employee stand out from the crowd and make them an asset to any organization.

Q: What are soft skills?

A: Soft skills are the personal attributes and qualities that enable an individual to interact effectively and harmoniously with other people. They are the skills that help you to communicate, collaborate, and work with others in a productive and efficient manner.

Q: Why are soft skills important?

A: Soft skills are important because they help employees to work together effectively and efficiently. They are the skills that enable employees to communicate effectively, collaborate, and work together to achieve common goals. Soft skills are also important because they help employees to build relationships with their colleagues and customers.

Q: How can you develop soft skills?

A: Soft skills can be developed through practice and experience. It is important to practice communication, problem-solving, teamwork, leadership, and interpersonal skills in order to develop them. It is also important to take the time to reflect on your experiences and learn from them. Soft skills can also be developed through formal education and training.

Q: What are the benefits of soft skills?

A: Soft skills have many benefits for both employers and employees. They help employers to create a productive and efficient workplace. They also help employees to develop their professional skills and abilities. Soft skills help employees to build relationships with their colleagues and customers. They also help employees to think critically, solve problems, and make decisions.

Q: How can soft skills help you in your career?

A: Soft skills can help you to stand out from the crowd and make you an asset to any organization. They are the skills that employers look for when hiring new employees. Soft skills can also help you to develop your professional skills and abilities. Soft skills can also help you to build relationships with your colleagues and customers. They are the skills that enable you to communicate effectively, collaborate, and work together to achieve common goals.

IMPORTANT COMMUNICATION SKILLS

THE IMPORTANCE OF COMMUNICATION SKILLS

Communication skills are essential for success in any field. Whether you are a student, a professional, or a business owner, having strong communication skills is essential for success. Communication skills are the ability to effectively convey and receive information, both verbally and non-verbally. They are the foundation of any successful relationship, whether it is with a customer, a colleague, or a friend.

Good communication skills are essential for any job, and they are especially important for those in leadership positions. Leaders must be able to effectively communicate their vision and goals to their team, and they must be able to listen to their team's ideas and feedback. Leaders must also be able to effectively communicate with customers, vendors, and other stakeholders.

TYPES OF COMMUNICATION SKILLS

There are many different types of communication skills, and each type has its own importance. Some of the most important communication skills include:

- Verbal Communication: Verbal communication is the ability to effectively communicate through spoken words. This includes the ability to listen, ask questions, and express ideas clearly.
- Non-Verbal Communication: Non-verbal communication is the ability to communicate without using words. This includes body language, facial expressions, and gestures.
- Written Communication: Written communication is the ability to effectively communicate through written words. This includes the ability to write clearly and concisely, as well as the ability to edit and proofread.
- Interpersonal Communication: Interpersonal communication is the ability to effectively communicate with others. This includes the ability to build relationships, resolve conflicts, and negotiate.

BENEFITS OF GOOD COMMUNICATION SKILLS

Good communication skills can have a positive impact on many aspects of life. Some of the benefits of good communication skills include:

- Improved Relationships: Good communication skills can help to build and maintain strong relationships with others.
- Increased Productivity: Good communication skills can help to increase productivity by ensuring that tasks are completed efficiently and effectively.
- Improved Problem-Solving: Good communication skills can help to identify and solve problems quickly and effectively.

- Increased Confidence: Good communication skills can help to increase confidence by allowing individuals to express themselves clearly and confidently.

HOW TO DEVELOP COMMUNICATION SKILLS

Developing communication skills is an ongoing process. Here are some tips for developing communication skills:

- Practice: The best way to develop communication skills is to practice. This can be done through role-playing, public speaking, or simply having conversations with others.
- Listen: Listening is an important part of communication. Make sure to listen carefully to what others are saying and ask questions to ensure that you understand.
- Be Open: Be open to feedback and criticism. This will help you to improve your communication skills and become a better communicator.
- Be Confident: Confidence is key when it comes to communication. Believe in yourself and your ability to communicate effectively.

CONCLUSION

Good communication skills are essential for success in any field. They are the foundation of any successful relationship, and they can have a positive impact on many aspects of life. Developing communication skills is an ongoing process, and it requires practice, listening, openness, and confidence. With the right attitude and effort, anyone can develop strong communication skills and become a better communicator.

Q: What are communication skills?

A: Communication skills are the ability to effectively convey and receive information, both verbally and non-verbally.

Q: What are the benefits of good communication skills?

A: The benefits of good communication skills include improved relationships, increased productivity, improved problem-solving, and increased confidence.

Q: How can I develop my communication skills?

A: The best way to develop communication skills is to practice. This can be done through role-playing, public speaking, or simply having conversations with others. Additionally, listening, being open to feedback and criticism, and having confidence are all important for developing communication skills.

Q: Are communication skills important for success?

A: Yes, communication skills are essential for success in any field. They are the foundation of any successful relationship, and they can have a positive impact on many aspects of life.

Q: What are some examples of communication skills?

A: Examples of communication skills include verbal communication, non-verbal communication, written communication, and interpersonal communication.

HOW TO IMPROVE YOUR CRITICAL THINKING SKILLS

Critical thinking is an essential skill for success in life. It is the ability to analyze and evaluate information, draw conclusions, and make decisions based on facts and evidence. It is a skill that can be developed and improved with practice. In this article, we will discuss how to improve your critical thinking skills and become a better problem solver.

WHAT IS CRITICAL THINKING?

Critical thinking is the process of analyzing and evaluating information in order to draw conclusions and make decisions. It involves using logic and reasoning to identify the strengths and weaknesses of an argument or idea. Critical thinking is an important skill for success in life, as it helps you to make better decisions and solve problems more effectively.

BENEFITS OF CRITICAL THINKING

Critical thinking can help you to become a better problem solver and make better decisions. It can also help you to think more clearly and objectively, and to develop better arguments and ideas. Additionally, it can help you to become more creative and open-minded, and to think outside the box.

HOW TO IMPROVE YOUR CRITICAL THINKING SKILLS

There are several ways to improve your critical thinking skills. Here are some tips to help you get started:

1. Read and Learn: Reading books, articles, and other materials can help you to gain knowledge and develop your critical thinking skills.
2. Ask Questions: Asking questions can help you to gain a better understanding of a topic or issue.
3. Analyze and Evaluate: Analyzing and evaluating information can help you to draw conclusions and make decisions.
4. Practice: Practicing critical thinking can help you to become more proficient in the skill.
5. Take Time to Reflect: Taking time to reflect on your thoughts and ideas can help you to gain a better understanding of a topic or issue.

DEVELOPING YOUR CRITICAL THINKING SKILLS

Developing your critical thinking skills requires practice and dedication. Here are some tips to help you get started:

1. Challenge Your Assumptions: Challenging your assumptions can help you to think more objectively and to develop better arguments and ideas.
2. Listen and Consider: Listening to others and considering their ideas can help you to gain a better understanding of a topic or issue.

3. Practice Problem Solving: Practicing problem solving can help you to become a better problem solver and make better decisions.
4. Take Time to Think: Taking time to think can help you to gain a better understanding of a topic or issue.
5. Seek Feedback: Seeking feedback from others can help you to gain a better understanding of a topic or issue.

CONCLUSION

Critical thinking is an essential skill for success in life. It is the ability to analyze and evaluate information, draw conclusions, and make decisions based on facts and evidence. It is a skill that can be developed and improved with practice. By reading, asking questions, analyzing and evaluating information, practicing problem solving, taking time to think, and seeking feedback, you can improve your critical thinking skills and become a better problem solver.

Q: What is critical thinking?

A: Critical thinking is the process of analyzing and evaluating information in order to draw conclusions and make decisions. It involves using logic and reasoning to identify the strengths and weaknesses of an argument or idea.

Q: What are the benefits of critical thinking?

A: Critical thinking can help you to become a better problem solver and make better decisions. It can also help you to think more clearly and objectively, and to develop better arguments and ideas. Additionally, it can help you to become more creative and open-minded, and to think outside the box.

Q: How can I improve my critical thinking skills?

A: There are several ways to improve your critical thinking skills. Reading books, articles, and other materials can help you to gain knowledge and develop your critical thinking skills. Asking questions, analyzing and evaluating information, practicing problem solving, taking time to think, and seeking feedback can also help you to improve your critical thinking skills.

Q: What is the best way to develop my critical thinking skills?

A: The best way to develop your critical thinking skills is to practice and dedicate yourself to the process. Challenging your assumptions, listening to and considering others' ideas, and taking time to reflect on your thoughts and ideas can help you to become a better problem solver and make better decisions.

Q: How long does it take to improve my critical thinking skills?

A: The amount of time it takes to improve your critical thinking skills depends on your dedication and practice. With consistent practice and dedication, you can expect to see improvements in your critical thinking skills over time.

THE IMPORTANCE OF VALUING YOUR MISTAKES

We all make mistakes. It's part of being human. But it's important to remember that mistakes can be valuable learning experiences. By valuing our mistakes, we can learn from them and grow as individuals.

MISTAKES ARE A NATURAL PART OF LIFE

No one is perfect. We all make mistakes. It's part of being human. We all have different experiences and perspectives, and we all make mistakes. It's important to remember that mistakes are a natural part of life.

VALUING YOUR MISTAKES CAN HELP YOU GROW

When we make mistakes, it's easy to get down on ourselves and feel like a failure. But it's important to remember that mistakes can be valuable learning experiences. By valuing our mistakes, we can learn from them and grow as individuals.

When we make mistakes, it's important to take the time to reflect on what went wrong and why. This can help us identify patterns and make changes to prevent similar mistakes in the future. It can also help us develop new skills and strategies to help us succeed.

VALUING YOUR MISTAKES CAN HELP YOU BUILD RESILIENCE

Making mistakes can be difficult and embarrassing. But it's important to remember that mistakes can help us build resilience. When we make mistakes, it's important to take the time to reflect on what went wrong and why. This can help us identify patterns and make changes to prevent similar mistakes in the future.

By valuing our mistakes, we can learn to be more resilient in the face of failure. We can learn to accept our mistakes and move on. We can also learn to be more open to feedback and criticism, which can help us grow and develop.

VALUING YOUR MISTAKES CAN HELP YOU DEVELOP SELF-AWARENESS

When we make mistakes, it's important to take the time to reflect on what went wrong and why. This can help us develop self-awareness. We can learn to recognize our strengths and weaknesses and identify areas where we need to improve.

By valuing our mistakes, we can learn to be more self-aware. We can learn to recognize our strengths and weaknesses and identify areas where we need to improve. We can also learn to be more open to feedback and criticism, which can help us grow and develop.

CONCLUSION

Making mistakes is a natural part of life. But it's important to remember that mistakes can be valuable learning experiences. By valuing our mistakes, we can learn from them and grow as individuals. We can learn to be more resilient in the face of failure and develop self-awareness. Valuing our mistakes can help us become better versions of ourselves.

Q: What is the importance of valuing mistakes?

A: Valuing mistakes can help us learn from them and grow as individuals. We can learn to be more resilient in the face of failure and develop self-awareness. Valuing our mistakes can help us become better versions of ourselves.

Q: How can valuing mistakes help us grow?

A: Valuing mistakes can help us identify patterns and make changes to prevent similar mistakes in the future. It can also help us develop new skills and strategies to help us succeed.

Q: How can valuing mistakes help us build resilience?

A: Valuing mistakes can help us learn to be more resilient in the face of failure. We can learn to accept our mistakes and move on. We can also learn to be more open to feedback and criticism, which can help us grow and develop.

Q: How can valuing mistakes help us develop self-awareness?

A: Valuing mistakes can help us develop self-awareness. We can learn to recognize our strengths and weaknesses and identify areas where we need to improve. We can also learn to be more open to feedback and criticism, which can help us grow and develop.

Q: What are some tips for valuing mistakes?

A: Some tips for valuing mistakes include taking the time to reflect on what went wrong and why, identifying patterns and making changes to prevent similar mistakes in the future, and being open to feedback and criticism.

THE IMPORTANCE OF PASSIVE INCOME

Passive income is a type of income that requires little to no effort to maintain. It is a form of income that is generated without actively working for it. Passive income is often referred to as "residual income" because it is generated from sources that are not actively managed. Passive income can be generated from a variety of sources, including investments, rental properties, and businesses.

Passive income is an important part of financial planning. It can provide a steady stream of income that can help to supplement other forms of income. It can also provide a cushion in the event of a job loss or other financial hardship. Passive income can also help to reduce the amount of taxes owed, as it is not subject to the same tax rates as earned income.

WHAT IS PASSIVE INCOME?

Passive income is income that is generated without actively working for it. It is generated from sources that are not actively managed. Examples of passive income include rental income from real estate investments, dividends from stocks and bonds, royalties from intellectual property, and income from businesses that require little to no effort to maintain.

BENEFITS OF PASSIVE INCOME

Passive income can provide a number of benefits. It can provide a steady stream of income that can help to supplement other forms of income. It can also provide a cushion in the event of a job loss or other financial hardship. Passive income can also help to reduce the amount of taxes owed, as it is not subject to the same tax rates as earned income.

TYPES OF PASSIVE INCOME

There are a variety of sources of passive income. These include rental income from real estate investments, dividends from stocks and bonds, royalties from intellectual property, and income from businesses that require little to no effort to maintain.

INVESTING IN PASSIVE INCOME

Investing in passive income can be a great way to generate a steady stream of income. It is important to do research and understand the risks associated with any investment. It is also important to diversify investments to reduce risk.

TAX IMPLICATIONS OF PASSIVE INCOME

Passive income is generally not subject to the same tax rates as earned income. This can provide a significant tax benefit. It is important to understand the tax implications of any passive income source before investing.

RISKS OF PASSIVE INCOME

Passive income can be a great way to generate a steady stream of income, but it is important to understand the risks associated with any investment. It is also important to diversify investments to reduce risk.

CONCLUSION

Passive income can be a great way to generate a steady stream of income. It can provide a number of benefits, including a cushion in the event of a job loss or other financial hardship. There are a variety of sources of passive income, including rental income from real estate investments, dividends from stocks and bonds, royalties from intellectual property, and income from businesses that require little to no effort to maintain. It is important to understand the risks associated with any investment and to diversify investments to reduce risk.

Q: What is passive income?

A: Passive income is income that is generated without actively working for it. It is generated from sources that are not actively managed. Examples of passive income include rental income from real estate investments, dividends from stocks and bonds, royalties from intellectual property, and income from businesses that require little to no effort to maintain.

Q: What are the benefits of passive income?

A: Passive income can provide a number of benefits. It can provide a steady stream of income that can help to supplement other forms of income. It can also provide a cushion in the event of a job loss or other financial hardship. Passive income can also help to reduce the amount of taxes owed, as it is not subject to the same tax rates as earned income.

Q: What are the types of passive income?

A: There are a variety of sources of passive income. These include rental income from real estate investments, dividends from stocks and bonds, royalties from intellectual property, and income from businesses that require little to no effort to maintain.

Q: What are the risks of investing in passive income?

A: Investing in passive income can be a great way to generate a steady stream of income, but it is important to understand the risks associated with any investment. It is also important to diversify investments to reduce risk.

Q: What are the tax implications of passive income?

A: Passive income is generally not subject to the same tax rates as earned income. This can provide a significant tax benefit. It is important to understand the tax implications of any passive income source before investing.

THE IMPORTANCE OF THINKING LOGICALLY

Logic is an essential part of our lives. It helps us make decisions, solve problems, and understand the world around us. But what is logic? How can we use it to our advantage? In this article, we'll explore the importance of thinking logically and how it can help us in our daily lives.

WHAT IS LOGIC?

Logic is the process of reasoning from one or more premises to a conclusion. It is a way of thinking that is based on facts and evidence, rather than emotion or opinion. Logic is used to determine the validity of an argument or statement. It is also used to identify logical fallacies, which are errors in reasoning that can lead to false conclusions.

Logic is an important part of critical thinking, which is the ability to analyze information and draw conclusions based on facts and evidence. Critical thinking is essential for making informed decisions and solving complex problems.

THE BENEFITS OF THINKING LOGICALLY

Thinking logically has many benefits. It can help us make better decisions, solve problems more efficiently, and understand complex concepts. Here are some of the benefits of thinking logically:

1. Improved Decision-Making: Thinking logically helps us make better decisions. By using logic, we can evaluate the pros and cons of a situation and make an informed decision.
2. Increased Problem-Solving Skills: Thinking logically can help us solve problems more efficiently. By using logic, we can identify the root cause of a problem and come up with a solution.
3. Improved Understanding: Thinking logically can help us understand complex concepts. By using logic, we can break down complex ideas into simpler parts and gain a better understanding of them.
4. Improved Communication: Thinking logically can help us communicate more effectively. By using logic, we can explain our ideas in a clear and concise manner.
5. Improved Critical Thinking: Thinking logically can help us develop our critical thinking skills. By using logic, we can analyze information and draw conclusions based on facts and evidence.

CONCLUSION

Logic is an essential part of our lives. It helps us make decisions, solve problems, and understand the world around us. Thinking logically has many benefits, including improved decision-making, increased problem-solving skills, improved understanding, improved communication, and improved critical thinking. By using logic, we can evaluate the pros and cons of a situation, identify the root cause of a problem, break down complex ideas, and communicate more effectively. Thinking logically is an important skill that can help us in our daily lives.

Q: What is logic?

A: Logic is the process of reasoning from one or more premises to a conclusion. It is a way of thinking that is based on facts and evidence, rather than emotion or opinion.

Q: What are the benefits of thinking logically?

A: The benefits of thinking logically include improved decision-making, increased problem-solving skills, improved understanding, improved communication, and improved critical thinking.

Q: How can logic help us make better decisions?

A: By using logic, we can evaluate the pros and cons of a situation and make an informed decision.

Q: How can logic help us solve problems?

A: By using logic, we can identify the root cause of a problem and come up with a solution.

Q: How can logic help us understand complex concepts?

A: By using logic, we can break down complex ideas into simpler parts and gain a better understanding of them.

LIFE SKILLS: WHAT THEY ARE AND HOW TO DEVELOP THEM

INTRODUCTION

Life skills are the abilities and knowledge that enable us to effectively manage our lives. They are the skills that help us to make the most of our lives and to reach our goals. Life skills are essential for success in all aspects of life, from personal relationships to professional success. They are the skills that help us to make decisions, solve problems, and manage our emotions.

Life skills are not something that we are born with; they must be developed over time. Developing life skills requires practice and dedication. It is important to understand that life skills are not something that can be learned overnight; they must be developed over time.

WHAT ARE LIFE SKILLS?

Life skills are the abilities and knowledge that enable us to effectively manage our lives. They are the skills that help us to make the most of our lives and to reach our goals. Life skills are essential for success in all aspects of life, from personal relationships to professional success. They are the skills that help us to make decisions, solve problems, and manage our emotions.

Life skills can be divided into three main categories: cognitive, emotional, and social. Cognitive skills are the skills that help us to think, reason, and make decisions. Emotional skills are the skills that help us to manage our emotions and to understand the emotions of others. Social skills are the skills that help us to interact with others and to build relationships.

HOW TO DEVELOP LIFE SKILLS

Developing life skills requires practice and dedication. It is important to understand that life skills are not something that can be learned overnight; they must be developed over time. Here are some tips for developing life skills:

1. Identify Your Goals: The first step in developing life skills is to identify your goals. What do you want to achieve in life? What do you want to be able to do? Identifying your goals will help you to focus on the skills that you need to develop.
2. Set a Plan: Once you have identified your goals, it is important to set a plan for achieving them. What steps do you need to take to reach your goals? What resources do you need? Setting a plan will help you to stay focused and motivated.
3. Practice: The best way to develop life skills is to practice them. Find opportunities to practice the skills that you need to develop. For example, if you want to develop your communication skills, practice having conversations with people.

4. Seek Feedback: It is important to seek feedback on your progress. Ask for feedback from people who can provide you with honest and constructive criticism. This will help you to identify areas where you need to improve.
5. Reflect: Take time to reflect on your progress. What have you learned? What have you achieved? Reflecting on your progress will help you to stay motivated and to identify areas where you need to improve.

CONCLUSION

Life skills are essential for success in all aspects of life. They are the skills that help us to make decisions, solve problems, and manage our emotions. Developing life skills requires practice and dedication. It is important to identify your goals, set a plan, practice, seek feedback, and reflect on your progress. With dedication and practice, you can develop the life skills that you need to reach your goals.

Q: What are life skills?

A: Life skills are the abilities and knowledge that enable us to effectively manage our lives. They are the skills that help us to make the most of our lives and to reach our goals. Life skills are essential for success in all aspects of life, from personal relationships to professional success.

Q: How can I develop life skills?

A: Developing life skills requires practice and dedication. It is important to identify your goals, set a plan, practice, seek feedback, and reflect on your progress. With dedication and practice, you can develop the life skills that you need to reach your goals.

Q: What are the three main categories of life skills?

A: Life skills can be divided into three main categories: cognitive, emotional, and social. Cognitive skills are the skills that help us to think, reason, and make decisions. Emotional skills are the skills that help us to manage our emotions and to understand the emotions of others. Social skills are the skills that help us to interact with others and to build relationships.

Q: What is the best way to practice life skills?

A: The best way to practice life skills is to find opportunities to use them in real-life situations. For example, if you want to develop your communication skills, practice having conversations with people.

Q: How long does it take to develop life skills?

A: Life skills are not something that can be learned overnight; they must be developed over time. The amount of time it takes to develop life skills will depend on the individual and the skills they are trying to develop.

HOW TO GET A GOOD JOB

Getting a good job is a goal that many people strive for. It can be a difficult process, but with the right preparation and attitude, it is possible to land a job that is both rewarding and fulfilling. In this article, we will discuss the steps you need to take to get a good job.

PREPARATION

The first step in getting a good job is to prepare yourself. This means taking the time to research the job market and the types of jobs that are available. You should also take the time to update your resume and make sure that it is up to date and accurate. Additionally, you should practice interviewing skills and make sure that you are prepared to answer any questions that may come up during the interview process.

NETWORKING

Networking is an important part of the job search process. You should take the time to reach out to people in your network and let them know that you are looking for a job. This can be done through social media, professional networking events, or even through word of mouth. Additionally, you should take the time to research companies and organizations that you may be interested in working for and reach out to them directly.

APPLYING

Once you have done your research and prepared yourself, it is time to start applying for jobs. You should take the time to read job postings carefully and make sure that you are applying for jobs that are a good fit for your skills and experience. Additionally, you should make sure that you are submitting a complete and accurate application. This includes a resume, cover letter, and any other documents that may be required.

INTERVIEWS

Once you have submitted your application, you may be invited to an interview. This is your chance to show the employer why you are the best candidate for the job. You should take the time to prepare for the interview and make sure that you are ready to answer any questions that may come up. Additionally, you should make sure that you are dressed appropriately and that you are prepared to discuss your qualifications and experience.

FOLLOW UP

After the interview, it is important to follow up with the employer. This can be done by sending a thank you note or email. Additionally, you should take the time to reach out to the employer and ask for feedback on your performance. This can help you to improve your interviewing skills and make sure that you are prepared for future interviews.

CONCLUSION

Getting a good job can be a difficult process, but with the right preparation and attitude, it is possible to land a job that is both rewarding and fulfilling. By taking the time to research the job market, network, apply, and prepare for interviews, you can increase your chances of getting a good job. Additionally, following up with the employer after the interview can help you to stand out from other candidates and increase your chances of getting the job.

Q: What is the best way to prepare for a job interview?

A: The best way to prepare for a job interview is to research the job market, practice interviewing skills, and make sure that you are prepared to answer any questions that may come up during the interview process. Additionally, you should make sure that you are dressed appropriately and that you are prepared to discuss your qualifications and experience.

Q: How can I make sure that my resume stands out?

A: To make sure that your resume stands out, you should take the time to update it and make sure that it is up to date and accurate. Additionally, you should make sure that it is tailored to the job that you are applying for and that it highlights your relevant skills and experience.

Q: What is the best way to network for a job?

A: The best way to network for a job is to reach out to people in your network and let them know that you are looking for a job. This can be done through social media, professional networking events, or even through word of mouth. Additionally, you should take the time to research companies and organizations that you may be interested in working for and reach out to them directly.

Q: How can I make sure that I am prepared for an interview?

A: To make sure that you are prepared for an interview, you should take the time to practice interviewing skills and make sure that you are prepared to answer any questions that may come up during the interview process. Additionally, you should make sure that you are dressed appropriately and that you are prepared to discuss your qualifications and experience.

Q: What is the best way to follow up after an interview?

A: The best way to follow up after an interview is to send a thank you note or email. Additionally, you should take the time to reach out to the employer and ask for feedback on your performance. This can help you to improve your interviewing skills and make sure that you are prepared for future interviews.

ALL ABOUT LOVE: A COMPREHENSIVE GUIDE

WHAT IS LOVE?

Love is a complex emotion that can be difficult to define. It is often described as a strong feeling of affection and attachment towards another person. It is a powerful emotion that can bring people together and create strong bonds. Love can be expressed in many different ways, such as through words, actions, and physical touch. It is often seen as a source of joy and happiness, but it can also be a source of pain and suffering.

TYPES OF LOVE

There are many different types of love, each with its own unique characteristics. These include romantic love, platonic love, familial love, and unconditional love.

Romantic love is the type of love that is often associated with relationships. It is a strong emotional connection between two people that is characterized by feelings of passion, desire, and intimacy. Platonic love is a type of love that is based on friendship and mutual respect. It is often seen as a strong bond between two people who care deeply for each other, but without any romantic or sexual feelings. Familial love is the type of love that exists between family members. It is a strong bond of affection and loyalty that is often seen as unconditional. Unconditional love is a type of love that is not based on any conditions or expectations. It is a type of love that is given freely and without any expectations of anything in return.

THE POWER OF LOVE

Love is a powerful emotion that can have a profound effect on people's lives. It can bring people together and create strong bonds that can last a lifetime. It can also be a source of joy and happiness, as well as a source of pain and suffering. Love can be a source of strength and courage, as well as a source of comfort and security. It can also be a source of inspiration and motivation.

THE BENEFITS OF LOVE

Love can bring many benefits to people's lives. It can bring joy and happiness, as well as a sense of security and comfort. It can also bring a sense of purpose and meaning to life. Love can also bring a sense of belonging and connection to others. It can also bring a sense of self-worth and confidence.

HOW TO FIND LOVE

Finding love can be a difficult and daunting task. It is important to remember that love is not something that can be forced or rushed. It is important to take the time to get to know someone and build a strong connection before committing to a relationship. It is also important to be open and honest with yourself and with the other person. It is also important to be patient and to trust that the right person will come into your life when the time is right.

HOW TO MAINTAIN LOVE

Maintaining a healthy and happy relationship takes work and dedication. It is important to communicate openly and honestly with your partner. It is also important to be supportive and understanding of each other's needs and feelings. It is also important to make time for each other and to show appreciation and affection. It is also important to be willing to compromise and to work together to resolve any conflicts that may arise.

HOW TO EXPRESS LOVE

Expressing love can be done in many different ways. It is important to find ways to show your partner that you care and appreciate them. This can be done through words, actions, and physical touch. It is also important to be open and honest with your feelings and to be willing to listen to your partner's feelings. It is also important to be supportive and understanding of each other's needs and feelings.

HOW TO OVERCOME CHALLENGES IN LOVE

Relationships can be challenging at times, but it is important to remember that all relationships have their ups and downs. It is important to be willing to work together to resolve any conflicts that may arise. It is also important to be open and honest with your feelings and to be willing to listen to your partner's feelings. It is also important to be supportive and understanding of each other's needs and feelings.

CONCLUSION

Love is a complex emotion that can bring many benefits to people's lives. It can bring joy and happiness, as well as a sense of security and comfort. It can also bring a sense of purpose and meaning to life. Finding and maintaining love can be a difficult and daunting task, but it is important to remember that it is worth the effort. It is important to take the time to get to know someone and build a strong connection before committing to a relationship. It is also important to be open and honest with yourself and with the other person. It is also important to be patient and to trust that the right person will come into your life when the time is right.

Q: What is love?

A: Love is a complex emotion that can be difficult to define. It is often described as a strong feeling of affection and attachment towards another person. It is a powerful emotion that can bring people together and create strong bonds.

Q: What are the different types of love?

A: The different types of love include romantic love, platonic love, familial love, and unconditional love.

Q: What are the benefits of love?

A: The benefits of love include joy and happiness, a sense of security and comfort, a sense of purpose and meaning to life, a sense of belonging and connection to others, and a sense of self-worth and confidence.

Q: How can I find love?

A: Finding love can be a difficult and daunting task. It is important to remember that love is not something that can be forced or rushed. It is important to take the time to get to know someone and build a strong connection before committing to a relationship. It is also important to be open and honest with yourself and with the other person.

Q: How can I maintain love?

A: Maintaining a healthy and happy relationship takes work and dedication. It is important to communicate openly and honestly with your partner. It is also important to be supportive and understanding of each other's needs and feelings. It is also important to make time for each other and to show appreciation and affection. It is also important to be willing to compromise and to work together to resolve any conflicts that may arise.

CODING FOR BEGINNERS: A COMPREHENSIVE GUIDE

Coding is a powerful tool that can be used to create amazing things. It is the language of computers and the foundation of modern technology. Whether you are a beginner or an experienced programmer, coding can be a great way to express yourself and create something unique. In this comprehensive guide, we will cover the basics of coding and provide you with the tools and resources you need to get started.

WHAT IS CODING?

Coding is the process of writing instructions for a computer to execute. It is the language of computers and the foundation of modern technology. Coding is used to create websites, apps, software, and other digital products. It is also used to automate tasks and create algorithms.

WHY LEARN TO CODE?

Learning to code can open up a world of possibilities. It can help you create amazing things, solve complex problems, and even make money. Coding can also help you develop valuable skills such as problem-solving, critical thinking, and creativity.

HOW TO GET STARTED WITH CODING

Getting started with coding can seem intimidating, but it doesn't have to be. There are many resources available to help you learn the basics and get started. Here are some tips to help you get started:

1. Choose a Programming Language: The first step is to choose a programming language. There are many different languages to choose from, so it's important to do your research and find the one that best suits your needs.
2. Find Resources: Once you've chosen a language, it's time to find resources to help you learn. There are many online tutorials, books, and courses available to help you get started.
3. Practice: The best way to learn is to practice. Try writing some code and see what happens. Don't be afraid to make mistakes, as this is part of the learning process.
4. Get Help: If you get stuck, don't be afraid to ask for help. There are many online forums and communities where you can get help from experienced coders.

CONCLUSION

Coding is a powerful tool that can be used to create amazing things. It is the language of computers and the foundation of modern technology. Whether you are a beginner or an experienced programmer, coding can be a great way to express yourself and create something unique. With the right resources and practice, anyone can learn to code and create amazing things.

Q: What is coding?

A: Coding is the process of writing instructions for a computer to execute. It is the language of computers and the foundation of modern technology.

Q: Why should I learn to code?

A: Learning to code can open up a world of possibilities. It can help you create amazing things, solve complex problems, and even make money.

Q: What programming language should I learn?

A: The best programming language to learn depends on your goals and needs. Do your research and find the language that best suits your needs.

Q: How can I get started with coding?

A: The best way to get started with coding is to find resources to help you learn. There are many online tutorials, books, and courses available to help you get started.

Q: Where can I get help with coding?

A: If you get stuck, don't be afraid to ask for help. There are many online forums and communities where you can get help from experienced coders.

SHOULD YOU HAVE AN EMERGENCY FUND?

When it comes to financial planning, having an emergency fund is one of the most important steps you can take. An emergency fund is a savings account that you can use to cover unexpected expenses, such as medical bills, car repairs, or job loss. Having an emergency fund can help you avoid taking on debt and can provide peace of mind in the event of an emergency. In this article, we'll discuss why you should have an emergency fund, how much you should save, and where to keep your emergency fund.

WHAT IS AN EMERGENCY FUND?

An emergency fund is a savings account that you can use to cover unexpected expenses. It's important to have an emergency fund because it can help you avoid taking on debt in the event of an emergency. An emergency fund should be separate from your regular savings account and should be easily accessible in case of an emergency.

WHY SHOULD YOU HAVE AN EMERGENCY FUND?

Having an emergency fund is important for several reasons. First, it can help you avoid taking on debt in the event of an emergency. If you don't have an emergency fund, you may be forced to take out a loan or use a credit card to cover unexpected expenses. This can lead to high interest rates and long-term debt.

Second, an emergency fund can provide peace of mind. Knowing that you have money set aside for unexpected expenses can help you sleep better at night. Finally, an emergency fund can help you avoid financial stress. Unexpected expenses can be stressful, but having an emergency fund can help you stay on top of your finances.

HOW MUCH SHOULD YOU SAVE?

The amount of money you should save in your emergency fund depends on your individual situation. Generally, it's recommended that you save at least three to six months' worth of living expenses. This means that if you were to lose your job, you would have enough money to cover your living expenses for three to six months.

If you're self-employed or have an irregular income, you may want to save more. It's also a good idea to save more if you have dependents or if you're in a high-risk profession.

WHERE SHOULD YOU KEEP YOUR EMERGENCY FUND?

When it comes to where to keep your emergency fund, it's important to choose an account that is easily accessible in case of an emergency. A high-yield savings account is a good option because it offers a higher interest rate than a regular savings account. You may also want to consider a money market account or a certificate of deposit.

CONCLUSION

Having an emergency fund is an important part of financial planning. An emergency fund can help you avoid taking on debt in the event of an emergency and can provide peace of mind. The amount of money you should save in your emergency fund depends on your individual situation, but it's generally recommended that you save at least three to six months' worth of living expenses. When it comes to where to keep your emergency fund, a high-yield savings account is a good option.

Q: What is an emergency fund?

A: An emergency fund is a savings account that you can use to cover unexpected expenses.

Q: Why should you have an emergency fund?

A: Having an emergency fund is important for several reasons. It can help you avoid taking on debt in the event of an emergency, provide peace of mind, and help you avoid financial stress.

Q: How much should you save in your emergency fund?

A: The amount of money you should save in your emergency fund depends on your individual situation, but it's generally recommended that you save at least three to six months' worth of living expenses.

Q: Where should you keep your emergency fund?

A: When it comes to where to keep your emergency fund, a high-yield savings account is a good option. You may also want to consider a money market account or a certificate of deposit.

Q: What should you do if you don't have an emergency fund?

A: If you don't have an emergency fund, it's important to start saving as soon as possible. Start by setting a goal and creating a budget to help you reach your goal. You may also want to consider cutting back on expenses or finding ways to increase your income.

UNDERSTANDING SUSTAINABLE INVESTMENTS

Sustainable investments are becoming increasingly popular as more and more people are looking for ways to make their money work for them while also making a positive impact on the environment. Sustainable investments are investments that are made with the intention of creating a positive environmental, social, and/or economic impact. These investments are often made in companies that are committed to sustainability, such as renewable energy, clean technology, and green building.

Sustainable investments are not only good for the environment, but they can also be good for your wallet. Sustainable investments can provide a steady stream of income, as well as the potential for long-term capital appreciation. In addition, sustainable investments can provide a hedge against inflation and can help diversify your portfolio.

WHAT ARE THE DIFFERENT TYPES OF SUSTAINABLE INVESTMENTS?

There are several different types of sustainable investments, each with its own unique benefits and risks.

Here are some of the most common types of sustainable investments:

1. Renewable Energy Investments: Renewable energy investments are investments in companies that are involved in the production of renewable energy, such as solar, wind, and geothermal. These investments can provide a steady stream of income, as well as the potential for long-term capital appreciation.
2. Clean Technology Investments: Clean technology investments are investments in companies that are involved in the development and production of clean technology, such as energy efficiency, water conservation, and waste management. These investments can provide a steady stream of income, as well as the potential for long-term capital appreciation.
3. Green Building Investments: Green building investments are investments in companies that are involved in the development and production of green building materials, such as energy-efficient windows, insulation, and roofing. These investments can provide a steady stream of income, as well as the potential for long-term capital appreciation.
4. Sustainable Agriculture Investments: Sustainable agriculture investments are investments in companies that are involved in the production of sustainable agriculture, such as organic farming and aquaculture. These investments can provide a steady stream of income, as well as the potential for long-term capital appreciation.
5. Impact Investing: Impact investing is a type of sustainable investment that focuses on investments

that have a positive social or environmental impact. These investments can provide a steady stream of income, as well as the potential for long-term capital appreciation.

WHAT ARE THE BENEFITS OF SUSTAINABLE INVESTMENTS?

Sustainable investments can provide a number of benefits, including:

1. Financial Returns: Sustainable investments can provide a steady stream of income, as well as the potential for long-term capital appreciation.
2. Diversification: Sustainable investments can help diversify your portfolio and provide a hedge against inflation.
3. Positive Impact: Sustainable investments can have a positive impact on the environment, society, and the economy.
4. Tax Benefits: Sustainable investments can provide tax benefits, such as tax credits and deductions.
5. Social Responsibility: Sustainable investments can help you feel good about where your money is going and how it is being used.

WHAT ARE THE RISKS OF SUSTAINABLE INVESTMENTS?

Sustainable investments can be risky, just like any other type of investment. Here are some of the risks associated with sustainable investments:

1. Market Risk: Sustainable investments can be subject to market risk, just like any other type of investment.

2. Regulatory Risk: Sustainable investments can be subject to regulatory risk, as regulations can change over time.
3. Liquidity Risk: Sustainable investments can be subject to liquidity risk, as they may not be as liquid as other types of investments.
4. Political Risk: Sustainable investments can be subject to political risk, as governments can change their policies over time.
5. Currency Risk: Sustainable investments can be subject to currency risk, as exchange rates can fluctuate over time.

CONCLUSION

Sustainable investments can be a great way to make your money work for you while also making a positive impact on the environment. Sustainable investments can provide a steady stream of income, as well as the potential for long-term capital appreciation. In addition, sustainable investments can provide a hedge against inflation and can help diversify your portfolio. However, sustainable investments can be risky, and it is important to understand the risks before investing.

Q: What is a sustainable investment?
A: A sustainable investment is an investment that is made with the intention of creating a positive environmental,

social, and/or economic impact. These investments are often made in companies that are committed to sustainability, such as renewable energy, clean technology, and green building.

Q: What are the different types of sustainable investments?

A: The most common types of sustainable investments are renewable energy investments, clean technology investments, green building investments, sustainable agriculture investments, and impact investing.

Q: What are the benefits of sustainable investments?

A: The benefits of sustainable investments include financial returns, diversification, positive impact, tax benefits, and social responsibility.

Q: What are the risks of sustainable investments?

A: The risks of sustainable investments include market risk, regulatory risk, liquidity risk, political risk, and currency risk.

ABOUT THE AUTHOR

I developed my passion for writing as a young person in the city of Philadelphia where all my dreams came alive. I always had my nose in a book and daydreamed about someday creating my own worlds. I have been crafting stories since I was old enough to hold a pencil. When I was twelve, I figured it out and decided I would be a writer when I grew up. My mission is to help others live their lives to the fullest and help others truly live their passion. My passion is helping people achieve the lift they envision.

I didn't grow up in an affluent home, I seen the obstacles my family faced with their finances. My family had very little savings and spent borrowed money on unnecessary expenses. When I'm not writing I can be found working out in my gym or cycling to keep in shape and listening to a variety of podcast

www.ingramcontent.com/pod-product-compliance
Lightning Source LLC
Chambersburg PA
CBHW060513130626
46553CB00002B/481